CHUCK WAGON HEYDAY

THE HISTORY & COLOR OF THE CHUCK WAGON

AT WORK

Best Wishes,

Tony Cano

CHUCK WAGON HEYDAY

THE HISTORY & COLOR OF THE CHUCK WAGON
AT WORK

Vividly depicting life around the chuck wagon during the heyday of the cattle trail drives and ranch roundups, this is the only published book focusing solely on the chuck wagon of the American West. It accurately portrays "Coosie" the distinctive trail cook and the important role he played, as well as his interactions with the colorful cowboys as they forged this significant segment of the West's history.

By
Tony Cano & Ann Sochat

Reata Publishing • Canutillo, Texas

DEDICATION

For Mike Dawson, a gentleman, a scholar, a man who has lived and adventured as a cowboy, and who has dedicated himself to preserving the wonderful heritage of the West.

TABLE OF CONTENTS

Books By
Tony Cano & Ann Sochat

Dutch Oven Cooking with Tony Cano

Echoes in the Wind
Ranch Recollections and Poetry

Chuck Wagon Heyday
The History & Color of the Chuck Wagon at Work

Cowhide 'n Calico
A Poet Looks at the West

Bandido
The True Story of Chico Cano, the Last Western Bandit
(Coming in April, 1997)

ABOUT THE AUTHORS

Tony Cano and Ann Sochat are writers who focus on that part of their heritage that they love best--the West--and the people who built and inhabited not only an area or a time period, but created an enduring place, so bold and free in its lifestyle, that modern inhabitants of the world still foster and revere it.

The authors perform and participate in cowboy symposiums and do seminars on Dutch oven cooking, and on roundups and life on the cattle trail. Among the professional associations that Cano and Sochat are active in are Western Writers of America, Texas Cowboy Poets, Western History Association, Westerners International, Academy of Western Artists, and Women Writing the West.

ACKNOWLEDGMENTS

Cover Illustration and the illustrations on page thirty and fifty-eight by David Ruiz, Jr.

Front cover design by Ann Sochat & Tony Cano.

Special thanks to Mr. John Doran, Principal, and Ms. Marg Wilson and her staff, Ms. Margie Zimmerman and Ms. Pat Molina, of Franklin High School's library in El Paso, Texas, for their unending assistance, understanding, and friendship.

Thanks also to Ms. Barbara Antebi of the Art Department at Franklin High School for the assistance given in the design and drawing of the chuck wagon art for the book.

INTRODUCTION

The modern day chuckwagon, though somewhat more elaborately equipped, is essentially the same in design and usage as it was back in the late 1800's. Its tradition and qualities remain pretty much the same today; the principles of coosie's responsibility remain intact to this day; the etiquette of the chuck wagon domain also has remained relatively unchanged. The situations, color, and camaraderie found around the chuck wagon remains to this day. Only the "windys" may have gotten bigger and better.

A significant difference is that modern day chuck wagon utilization is restricted to large ranch roundups instead of the trail drives of yesteryear. Large ranches in the West still must round up thousands of cattle and get them ready to go to market, although now big trucks come in and load them up and transport them to the large beef market areas.

Those large roundups of yesteryear usually began around April 15th. and would last until the first of December. Though there were customarily two major roundups, spring and fall, one actually ran into the other with interrelated and necessary tasks carried on in-between. Coosie was kept quite busy feeding and caring for all those cowboys for some three-quarters of the year.

The majority of big ranches in West Texas were built soon after 1885 when barbed wire fences were constructed around the huge grazing ranges. The enormous number of cattle, some ranches having up to fifty or sixty thousand cattle, were now kept confined, and by 1888, the open-range roundups and trail drives were destined to bite the dust and blow away like a tumbling tumbleweed. The reality of the trail drives were forever gone, but they would inspire a new mythology in the retelling of their adventures.

The great cowboy experience had begun in 1866 and had lasted until shortly after 1885. It endured but a short period of time, but left a lasting impression and legacy of the history of the West. Right smack in the middle of the whole affair was the chuck wagon, nerve center of the outfit, and its cook, *cocinero,* or coosie for short, who was the backbone of the trail drives. Coosie was destined to become an integral cast member of Western lore and its heritage.

Little did the father of the chuck wagon, the inventor himself, Charles "Chuck" Goodnight realize at the time the enormous significance his wagon would carry into the future of the West and its mystique. He was only trying to feed his cowboys....

Part 1

WHY CATTLE DRIVES BEGAN
COOK AND COWBOY ORIGINS

The cowboy was responsible for the great awakening of the West as we know it today. Much can be said about the building of the West and the role played by the cowboy and the supporting cast of characters who enacted the vigorous dramas which were replayed throughout the Western states. Grade B movies, television series, documentaries, and factually-written screenplays have provided stereotypes of the working ranch hand, the cattle baron, the sheriffs, outlaws, settlers, and merchants who each served an important function in expanding the American frontier. These stereotypes are composites of the many actual characters who peopled the towns and open spaces of the West. While they may exaggerate some features, they are true to many of the humorous and dramatic elements of these characters. The trail drive period of cattle ranching is one of the most accurately portrayed, and most notably the cook, *cocinero,* or coosie for short was destined to become an integral cast member of Western Americana.

Several events and passages of time were necessary for the evolution of the ranch cook or *cocinero* as he was known, due to his Spanish roots.

The cowboy's origins go back to the Spanish and the first "cow hunters" who came to the New World in late 1519 with Hernan Cortes. Wherever the Spaniards went in the New World, they always took cattle and horses with them. In February of 1521, a vessel arrived in Mexico from Spain, loaded with a mixture of cattle and bulls. These cattle were intended to feed the conquistadores in their quest for the gold rumored to be in abundance in the New World. While the conquistadores might have been willing to take care of their horses, they were basically fighting men. Taking care of cattle was considered to be "beneath" them, so special "herders," were brought along to fill that necessary position. The vaquero or cowboy who tamed the Western frontier was a metamorphosis from these first herders, from conquistadores who stayed on in the New World, and from the native mestizo who had intermarried with the Spaniards.

This *vaquero* evolved from the herders and was the basis of the cowboy as we know him today. He was responsible for crafting the legacy of skills, cowboy language, and style that would live on in the new American West character that would become famous around the nation and the world after only humble beginnings on the Texas and Mexico frontier. He was a proud man who wore his *espuelas*, spurs, with pride, signaling in sight and musical jingles to all around, that he was a man who worked with cattle. Here was a man who would do any job on the ranch, as long as it was on horseback. He would never walk anywhere if he could ride his horse, no matter the distance.

So the Spaniard was important in impacting the future of North America in more ways than those defined by their expeditions northward. Cortes himself created the first ranch in America when he went into the cattle business, establishing a big spread he called *Cuernavaca*, or "Cow Horn."

But the land was vast and mostly unpopulated, and from the original cattle and horses brought on the ships, many of the cattle found their way to the free range and multiplied to the point that there were thousands of cattle roaming wild and free on the Mexican range. These cattle, unlike the modern day cattle, were quite wild, actually aggressively dangerous and difficult to control, especially in large herds. It was these cattle that were the basis for the great *hacienda* ranches which sprung up when the Spanish nobles took their tremendously large land grants and began ranching operations. Though the Spanish explorers had failed to find the abundant riches they had hoped for, they had found an alternative way to riches beyond belief.

Slowly the ranches and their livestock found their way to northern Mexico, and by the early 1800's had actually crossed into what is now Texas and New Mexico, where large land grants helped spring up even more sprawling ranches. Texas, with thousands of miles of grasslands, was destined to be the motherland of the cattle industry.

The cattle business prospered until the Civil War broke out in 1861, and a temporary halt to any further development occurred. Many Texans went off to fight for the Southern cause.

The cattle, left to fend for themselves, out of necessity learned how to survive without much water or food, and became wilder and especially more productive than ever. In the absence of the cowboys, the herds had tremendously increased in number. There were now to be found an unbelievable four to six million wild mavericks--unbranded animals belonging to no one-- roaming the vast Texas ranges. All these mavericks needed was someone to come in and put their brand on them and claim them, which was easier said than done.

The Civil War was over on April 9, 1865, and many soldiers from both the North and the South had no home to go back to, so they went west in search of adventure and fortune. There were also large numbers of freed slaves, mostly with the army cavalry, who came west and were eventually mustered out of the army while out west. Most of these Negroes stayed and became cowboys, eventually numbering up to fifteen percent of the total cowboys.

Newly converted cowboys came from all over Mexico and now the United States as well. The American cowboys were of different cultural backgrounds, some of them being rather new to this country. Cowboying would give them a common denominator. The men who joined this new fraternity, almost to a man, shared three basic characteristics: youth, a lack of any family, and a hankering for the freedom that comes in traveling light, all their earthly belongings being carried with them when they arrived.

The vastness of the Texas plains and the freedom and adventure of the cowboy's life was the strong magnet needed to stir the imaginations of young men throughout the country. Cowboys who went on the trail were considered heroes by the rest of the country, who by now had created the cowboy mystique and had elevated them to national attention.

Even more immigrants came from many sections of the United States and various parts of the world, most notably from Ireland, England, Mexico, and some of the Scandinavian countries. Most of these immigrants would in time prove to be capable cowboys, ranchers, and farmers.

These men were rich and poor, city boys and farm boys, educated and uneducated, millionaire's sons, had a profession or no profession at all. There were even men running away from the law or from some unhappy woman, and young boys barely able to reach the stirrups found themselves working as cowboys.

Not all of the newfangled cowboys lasted long enough to see a trail drive all the way through. The hard work took only a few days to disillusion many of them. Some began work on the first of the week and quit before the end of the same week. They realized ever so abruptly that the hard, grueling, and unending grind was not as interesting and romantic as they had expected or had been led to believe.

The man directly responsible for the birth of the chuck wagon, Charles "Chuck" Goodnight, began gathering his herd of cattle in 1866. Goodnight was only thirty years of age at the time, but because of the demanding life of the Texas frontier, had seasoned into a well-known cattle man and was mentally and physically adapted to this way of life. His first venture at ranching up near Pueblo, Colorado, had not proven to be so profitable, and nearing bankruptcy, he had to find another avenue to pursue. Goodyear was known to lecture his fellow cattlemen about being decisive and taking action when circumstances dictated it. He was now at a point where he faced the testing of his espoused theories: he had reached that fork of the road where he could keep on going in one direction as he had been doing, or go in the other direction and open new frontiers. His new frontier ran north.

That spring, Goodnight had managed to gather only a small herd of some one thousand head of cattle fit for driving on the trail. Up to this time, the cattle drives had been almost exclusively to the southern states, as they were destitute for beef, and the Confederacy needed to feed its army. Money was now short in supply to the south, and Goodnight decided that the better choice was to go north and west to new markets. He felt that the newly-found mining riches supplied the money to pay for his cattle, and he could fetch a good price per head as well. Additional factors were that the railroads had to feed their construction crews, the U.S. Army had troops all over the West to feed, and the federal government had begun providing beef to the Indians who were being confined to reservations. The western cattle industry, out of necessity, was about to boom, with the new *vaquero*--cowboy--right smack in the middle.

Cattle were worth no more than four dollars a head in the impoverished and war-torn South, but those same cattle would bring forty dollars or more up north. If one could assemble a herd of one thousand head, worth four thousand dollars, and turn them around for forty thousand dollars...well, it was more money than a man could earn in a lifetime.

This was Goodnight's way of escaping the turbulent border of Texas and the problems of the South. He would go north and set up his operations within the vast expanses of open ranges filled with abundance of grass and water for his beef.

An industrial revolution was taking place back east, and beef was needed to feed all the people flocking to the cities to work in the mills and factories. The problem was how to get all those cattle to market. The Mississippi steamboats could not carry many cattle, and the railroad had not reached out to Texas yet. The nearest railroad heads were to the north in Missouri and Kansas.

The only foreseeable way to get the cattle to market was going to be to walk them all the way up the established cattle trails. Eventually, five major trails were established, the Goodnight-Loving Trail and the Chisholm Trail being the two most heavily-traveled ones of the bunch.

The Goodnight-Loving trail began in central Texas, went due west, and after crossing the Pecos River, headed north through New Mexico Territory, crossing the Red River and Canadian River. From there, it advanced up into Colorado to the Pueblo and Denver railheads, then on up into Wyoming to Cheyenne. The Cheyenne railhead was probably the most important station due to the fact that the Union Pacific R.R. was the only available line transporting cattle to western markets from that point. The Chicago & Northern R. R. went east to Chicago, from where eastern markets were served.

The Chisholm Trail began in south Texas and went up through central Texas past Fort Worth, north up through the Oklahoma Indian Territory, and on to Kansas.

Both these cattle trails were long and hard with many obstacles, both man-made and natural. Many cowboys lost their lives to stampedes, raging rivers, Indians, rustlers, and farmers opposing their passage through their lands.

The farmers in Missouri were especially set against having the Texas cattle go through their state as they claimed that Texas cattle carried diseases which were killing off their own herds, which were not immune to those diseases. More than one cattle drive was forcibly turned back at the Missouri border.

These were problems that Goodnight would have to deal with and work through if he was going to succeed in his plan to move his cattle to the beef-hungry populace who had the cash to pay. Goodnight had the first essentials: cattle, cowboys, buyers, destinations. He had to figure out the logistics for moving those cattle through unsettled territory for an extended trail drive and figure out an expedient way to carry all the necessary food and equipment with which to feed the hungry cowboys who would be herding the cattle.

Part 2

INVENTING THE CHUCK WAGON

In previous trips where Goodnight had driven cattle south, things had not worked out so well, and the men had been disgruntled and unhappy with the lack of proper food. These cowboys now demanded a real cook and good "chuck" as food came to be known. Legend has it that the name "chuck" came from Charles "Chuck" Goodnight, since he was responsible for the "chuck" wagon that provided the food.

Everyone knew that a good *cocinero* had to be able to carry large amounts of food and related items to be able to sustain the men for months at a time. No one had yet conceived an efficient method for doing this. After conferring with his cook, Goodnight designed the missing ingredient: the "food wagon," as he first called his first wagon.

A very durable wagon was a must, as it would be loaded to its maximum weight of up to two tons and would be constantly on the move, day in and day out for months at a time. It would be so heavy that when fully loaded, it required four mules, and often up to six mules, to supply the power necessary to transport the wagon over the difficult terrain often found on the trail.

Goodnight found what he needed when he heard that the army was willing to sell some of its overstocked government wagons. Some of those wagons, used for hauling ammunition and supplies, had a heavy metal foundation running gear and broad-tiered wheels. He chose one with wide-gauge wheels which he felt should withstand most any terrain, not topple over as easily, and would also carry more weight than normal wagons, which he required.

Goodnight took his newly-purchased wagon over to a wagon company in Parker County. There, he ordered it completely refurbished with modifications designed exclusively by himself from the ground up.

Charles "Chuck" Goodnight diligently jumped in and worked side-by-side with the wagon company workers, overseeing each and every minute detail. The main wagon bed was constructed of the hardest wood available at the time, seasoned bois d'arc. The wooden axles running beneath the bed were replaced with iron axles, which were more durable. To maintain the new strong axles, Goodnight took to using tallow instead of the more common tar to grease them.

Goodnight himself designed and had constructed for the back of the wagon bed the first "food" box ever seen. Its array of compartments, cubbyholes, and drawers which would store everything from food stuffs to medicinal whiskey were numerous. The hinged lid protecting these drawers could be let down from the top on its centered, single wooden leg and thus shape the cook's work-table. One of the most important and most-used pieces of equipment had to be the coffee grinder which was attached near the chuck box.

Before the wagon was even completed, the wagon company owner had already coined its new name, "Chuck's wagon," later shortened to "chuck wagon." And the food box was appropriately renamed the "chuck box." By the time the first mules were hitched to the new wagon, everyone already knew it and referred to it as the chuck wagon. The name stuck.

Beneath the chuck box was the boot, which was another large compartment where all the heavy cast-iron kettles, pans, and skillets were stored. The wagon bed just in front of the chuck box and directly behind the driver was used to carry the rolled-up bed rolls belonging to the hands, extra supplies of flour, bacon, coffee, beans, canned goods, dried fruit, rice, flour, molasses (lick, as cowboys referred to it), sugar, and other necessary staples. A conscientious cook would always double-sack each individual staple to prevent any content loss in case of a tear to the sack.

All of the items on the wagon were protected from the elements by a heavy canvas held up by Bentwood bows attached to the sides of the wagon. This was a snug place to sleep in foul weather and was a privilege reserved exclusively for the cook. The grain for the team of mules or horses was packed in the front end under the driver's springed seat.

On one side of the wagon was attached a large wooden barrel for the water supply, which was enough for roughly two days. To balance the heavy weight, a large tool box was attached to the opposite side of the wagon. This sturdy box contained branding irons, horseshoeing equipment, an ax, shovel, pick, and hammers and other such necessary tools.

A dried cowhide or heavy canvas known as a *cuna* or cradle was hung, hammock fashion, underneath the wagon to carry the wood fuel where wood was scarce. It was also a convenient way of keeping the wood dry in wet weather. Nothing was more frustrating than having to try to start a fire with wet wood. It was customary for all the hands to help in keeping the *cuna* loaded with wood to be used by the cook. Like many other Spanish names associated with the ranching industry, *cuna* too was soon Americanized to *cooney*.

It didn't take long to come up with some protection from the elements in the way of a long fly of canvas stretched from the wagon and covering the cook's working area. This area was also shared with the hands, and in inclement weather, they would bunch up, huddling under the fly's protection to take their meals without rain getting into their plates.

An integral second wagon, separate from the chuck wagon, was known as the hoodlum's wagon. This wagon carried odds and ends such as water, medicines, spare saddles, and wood to be used for cooking when trees were not available on the trail, as well as other countless necessities for both the men and the stock. The extra branding irons and necessary tools, as well as extra grain for the teams were also packed in. Not all outfits had the second wagon, and thus they would just have to load up the chuck wagon to capacity.

The finished chuck wagon was a heavy, ironed-up affair, but it was actually light running due mostly in part to the high narrow wheels, narrow tires, and a wider-than-normal gauge. The wide gauge was necessary because the wagon often was top-heavy, and when navigating steep hills or rough deep gullies would otherwise risk rolling over.

It is speculated that the first provision ever to go on board was an ample supply of Arbuckle's coffee. The brand name *Arbuckle's* was synonymous with coffee and was a blessing, because until the Arbuckle brothers of Pittsburgh developed their special roasting and coating techniques in 1865, ranchers had been compelled to go to the trouble of roasting their own coffee beans. It was a tedious and time-consuming task, and many a skillet full of roasting beans had been burned.

John and Charles Arbuckle came up with a special egg and sugar-glaze coating technique that kept the coffee beans tasty for long periods of time. This glaze sealed in the flavor and freshness and thus became popular with the ranchers and cow camps. Though the beans still had to be put through the coffee bean grinder, they no longer had to be roasted.

Arbuckle's company popularized the use of merchandise coupons that could be redeemed for a variety of merchandise, including aprons, watches, window curtains, Western story books, and even a .32-caliber revolver. It is interesting to note that the name *Arbuckle* also became a derogatory and scoffing term for a greenhorn cowboy, who supposedly was obtained with trading stamps given away with the coffee.

A highly sought-after bonus stick of peppermint candy was also included in each one-pound package of Arbuckle's' coffee. When the cook needed some help in grinding the coffee beans, he would call out, "Who wants the candy?" and he was always assured of getting several volunteers. Candy was not readily available on the range, and some of the toughest hands in the West would practically fight for the privilege of cranking the coffee grinder as a means of being awarded the coveted candy. A wise cook wouldn't let the volunteer have the peppermint until the whole package of coffee beans had been ground up.

Second to be loaded into the chuck wagon, more than likely, was the keg of sourdough needed in the preparation of the biscuits and bread which were so much a staple food of the cowboys. The sourdough keg was usually tied to the outside of the wagon where the heat could keep the contents in proper fermenting temperature. If the weather would turn cold, then the keg was kept under the protection of the wagon bed under all those bed rolls to keep it warm.

Charles Goodnight had learned of sourdough from his mother years before, and although the sourdough mixture had been around for ages at ranches, Goodnight is credited with being the first to take it along on the trail.

Piece by piece, with much thought and consultation, the evolution of the chuck wagon came about. Thus, Goodnight ingeniously created the vehicle to solve what had been his worrying question about driving the cattle northward.

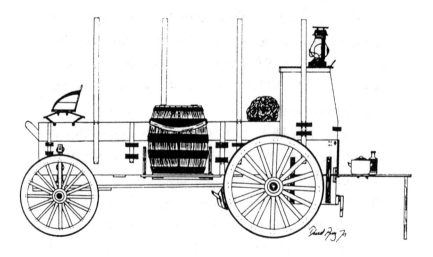

Part 3

THE ROLE OF THE COOK

The challenge Goodnight now encountered was having to select and hire the cook to man his newly-constructed chuck wagon. A cook at ranch headquarters was not usually a problem, as the women would mostly do the cooking and caring for all of his cowboys. But to ask a woman to go out on the trail drive with all the lack of comforts and with the tremendous hardships and danger was too much to consider. Not that the hardy women found in the West were unequal to these rigors. That women were not welcome on the trail drives was due to cowboy attitudes. The belief (probably quite justifiable and based on experience) was that a single woman out on the trail for such an extended period of time would cause problems, rivalries, and fighting among the trail hands. The trail boss also did not want to worry about the cavalier attitude of the cowboys if trouble occurred. The cowboy acted almost instinctively to save a dangerous situation on the trail drives, generally without regard for his own life. The cattle and supplies had to be the main concerns, but if a woman were present, that same cowboy might jeapordize cattle and all to come to her rescue. The theory also was that down time was scarce enough on the trail without the cowboys having to worry about being clean or shaving or about their appearance, which would be a natural inclination in a woman's presence. So a man was designated cook, and after a crash course from the women in preparing meals, was now supposedly ready to feed the hungry "outfit" as the group of cowboys as a whole connected with the trail crew was known.

Selection of the cook was no simple matter, and many requisites came into the picture. Most cooks were middle-aged or older working cowboys who, due to physical limitations, no longer could take the rigors of the day-to-day dangerous job of working the cattle. The lamentable truth was that these men knew nothing else except cowboying, and the prospect of having to go out and try to make a living at another occupation was scary, to say the least.

Many an old cowboy made the transition to cook being only too happy to be able to earn his pay same as the other cowboys. Being able to tag along with his cronies and join in the adventure was a big plus. It was better than staying behind at the main ranch and being bunkhouse chef, cooped up in an indoor kitchen with four walls and maybe one little window to let in the outdoors.

He much preferred the outdoors with all the hardships of, but not limited to: dust, heat or cold, rain, wind, and all that hard work. His job as cook on the range was twice as demanding as it was back at the ranch headquarters, but more exhilarating.

Obviously, there were positive conditions he left behind by choosing to go on the trail. Away from the ranch, he didn't have a large wood-burning stove and a big woodpile to go with it, customarily chopped and stacked by some of the ranch help. He didn't have a plentiful supply of water from the well or windmill (some ranches even had a hand pump in the kitchen area itself).

He left behind the pantry and storerooms with their ample shelves and storage bins, and the vegetable garden which could be found at most ranches to supply the ranch house kitchens. For sure, he couldn't take the table and chairs along, much less his comfortable bed. He also left behind the chickens which provided the poultry meat with which to prepare his finger-licking-good fried chicken, not to mention the fresh eggs, hen fruit, they produced in ready supply.

These inconveniences were balanced by the freedom, the camaraderie, the salary, and, yes, the power that went with the trail cook's position.

As time progressed, the trail cook's profession was sufficiently recognized to have a standard wage scale. He became an indispensable hand and was paid the wage of a top hand. When ordinary hands were getting $30.00 a month, wagon cooks got $40.00. This was considered very good pay, considering that he received room and board in addition to this salary,

Literate men, especially cooks who could read and write, commanded up to four times the pay of ordinary hands. These literate 'pokes helped keep ranch records and helped with the correspondence of both the ranch and the other hands. The cook at ranch headquarters, known as "bunkie," was more of an aristocrat and found himself on the same wage scale as the trail boss or the ranch foreman, *caporal*. This fact alone exemplified the importance of the cook.

Often, a down-and-out cowboy would stray into camp looking for a job and encounter a situation where the present cook had asked for his time and was leaving the outfit, either because the law was closing in on him or because he had endured just about enough ribbing about his cooking. The newly-arrived cowboy would be hired with open arms. Hell, all he had to have was some sort of rudimentary knowledge of cooking, and he was automatically qualified. It was either the unproven new cowboy or one of the hands being promoted to head cook, an honor most of them spurned, especially if the cook had been driven off, since they were aware of how nasty cowboys could be about the food they ate.

Any time there was any indication of the current cook being let go because of bad cooking: "the gravy was so tough it had to be cut with a knife in little squares before you could eat it," it was only a matter of time before he was fired. When this would occur, the cowboys would scatter and make themselves scarce lest the boss happen to see one of them not working to his satisfaction or expectations, and he might very well be quickly "promoted" to make-do cook.

"Out of sight, out of mind," became the favorite saying for any cowboy trying to avoid being volunteered into any job not having to do with riding a horse.

Every aspect of the trail drive was directly connected to the *cocinero*. The morale of the men depended upon him. A poor, sloppy, dirty, unshaven, and grouchy cook would almost always assure bad morale and problems with the cowboys. On the other hand, a good-natured, clean, and pleasant cook made for a smooth-running crew no matter what the work entailed. Morale would be sky-high, and cowboys would fight to keep their jobs.

If a rancher wanted to ensure top hands for his trail drive, a good cook was the attracting lure to get them. The first question a cowboy would ask when he was considering joining an outfit was "How's the grub?" Neighboring ranches would get the word of a good cook, and soon cowboys would be trying to hitch on to the well-fed outfit. Next to his horse, the cowboy's most urgent need was good food--lots of it, on a regular basis.

The majority of the cooks were clean and had pride in their work and equipment. Their camp was organized and clean, as they were themselves. The circumstances of existence on the trail left the men with a constant need for soap and water. The cowboy could be tolerated for his ablutionary shortcomings, but not the cook. There was nothing worse and more intolerable than a grubby, smelly, unkempt cook with his dirty hands all over the food.

While the cowboys were not that fastidious about their own persons, they were quite particular in expecting the cook to maintain clean personal habits, and one who didn't was frowned upon. One not-so-clean cook made a comment about the meal that he had cooked being fit for angels. A cowboy wryly rejoined that he had never heard of angels as being flat-nosed, grunting beings with circles at their tails, instead of at their heads.

On the trail, cooks would sometimes, for whatever reason, have to be replaced without delay and with haste, as three meals a day had to be supplied at whatever cost and with whatever means were available. The loss of a cook was a serious situation, unlike the loss of a cowboy who could be more easily replaced. Usually a cowboy with any rudimentary knowledge of the art of cooking was "promoted" to the rank of cook until another could be located.

If the trail boss was in a democratic mood, he would take out straws of different lengths and have each man draw his fate. Of course, the cowboy left holding the short straw won the distinction of camp cook. If the boss had it in for a particular cowboy for whatever reason, he would more than likely forgo the democratic process and simply elect the new "volunteer" recruit. It was beneficial to be on the good side of the boss at times like this.

Sometimes a good cook who felt he was not appreciated by his peers would ask the trail boss for a few days off to attend to some personal business. The boss had to let him go because he knew if he didn't, the cook would go anyway. The cook would more often than not "recommend" to the trail boss which one of the cowboys would make a good substitute cook. This was only one of various methods utilized by the cook to get even with that particular cowboy and have the last laugh. Believe me, after a week without the main cook in residence, the outfit was more than happy to mend its ways and welcome the permanent cook back with open arms.

The tale is told of one such substitute cook who decided to make some rice, as he felt it was very simple to prepare. Being that this was to be his first attempt at cooking rice, he was unaware of its ability to swell. As a result, the beginning quantity of rice thrown into the pot produced enough cooked rice to fill quite a few containers, and the cowboys had to eat enormous amounts of the rice for the next three days. The bewildered cook even threw in a few raisins, some sugar and cinnamon, mixed it up good and proper, and called it dessert. Colorful nicknames often arose from just such fiascos.

Many cowboys would be very unhappy to lose a good cook and have him be replaced with a not-so-capable one. But, cowboy be forewarned, it was an unwritten rule of the range that anyone complaining or criticizing the substitute's cooking results would immediately be handed over the cook's flour-sack apron and be designated as new cook in residence. He would be destined to hold that position until the next cowboy complained, or until the full-time cook's position was filled.

The cook was always under considerable pressure to meet the demands of the preparation of three rib-sticking meals for the hands. Weather remained a factor to be contended with in his job. On one day, he might be trying to cook a meal in poring rain for ten to twenty men, with a shortage of food or dry wood. Another day, the water barrels might be running low, and water consumption had to be carefully watched. Wind caused havoc with the fires, spreading the heat every which way but under the pots. If the cook's job was difficult in calm weather, it was a nightmare in the windy and dusty climates the outfit usually navigated. It was a constant fight to keep dust out of the food, and maintaining a good, steady, hot fire was difficult when it was windy and rainy and the wood was mostly wet. Then he had to contend with the sandstorms blowing fine or gritty particles into his eyes and into his meals. Extreme heat made his job of cooking over hot coals almost unbearable. Extreme cold would slow the baking and cooking process of the Dutch ovens.

It's no wonder that most of them were known as "grouchy old men." Cowboys swore that all range cooks were cranky and ornery, to say the least. "Very temperamental and a breed of their own," voiced one cowboy, under condition of anonymity.

Most of the cowboys tolerated the cook's shortcomings and tried to stay on his good side for obvious dietary reasons. When the cook was having a bad day, the hands would stay out of his way. According to an old saying, "Only a fool argues with a skunk, a mule, or a cook."

The cook had a way of getting even with the hands when necessary to keep them in their proper place. There was a lighter side to the cook though, as some were not without their quick wit and humor and had a keen repartee to boot. When pushed too far, the cook could become quite vicious with his witty disposition, perhaps because of his outlook on life itself. He could ridicule and paralyze the defenses of most 'pokes, leaving them at a loss for words.

Take the incident of one cowboy who criticized coosie's cooking. The cowboy was silenced with the cook's quick wit: "Well, if you weren't such a rotten card player, or if you paid off your gambling debts, you could go into town and get a break from my cooking, 'stead of having to stay out here an' hide in my wagon every time someone from town shows up!" Most of the cowboy's good-natured ribbing was geared towards coosie's sourdough biscuits, because they knew this to be a touchy subject, practically guaranteed to get results. This didn't always work on the more experienced and wise cook who took it all in good humor. He knew there were some trail hands who relished laughter derived at his expense, and that the more he showed his displeasure, the more ribbing he would get.

The cook had one thing going for him...he was indispensable; he was the uncrowned king. Coosie was a jack-of-all trades--he was the doctor, dentist, psychologist, veterinarian, mediator, barber, sewer of buttons, and giver of advice. For the very young cowboy (and there were many) away from his home for the first time, coosie served as unwilling surrogate mother.

Coosie also served as instructor for those essential areas of information which the cowhand lacked. The majority of the new hands were already able to tell the time of day according to the position of the sun in the sky and the shadows produced by the sun during the course of the day. However, the problem of telling time was complicated when the western horizon swallowed the sun....

Coosie had to show the greenhorns how to tell time by the Big Dipper in the night sky. "The two end stars of the cup will always line up and point to the North Star," coosie schooled the dudes, drawing the dipper's design with a stick on the sand, and using a rock to designate the location of the North Star. The Big Dipper up there makes a complete circle around the North Star every twenty-four hours, and you can tell the time by its relative position in the sky."

He was also sort of a sheriff, keeping the peace as best he could. After being on the trail for a few weeks, the men's tempers would be strained, and they would begin to get on each other's nerves...in stepped coosie, sometimes even confiscating all firearms for the duration of the drive. He was actually third in command behind *el segundo,* the cowboy who was second in command to the trail boss. All this gave him tremendous power.

Thus, the cook passed the greater part of the day hurrying from one role to the next to accommodate the needs of the men on the trail. The early evening was a time for the cook to settle down, and his chores became somewhat lighter. He would finally get to enjoy a leisurely smoke or some chewing tobacco, usually preferring Star Navy or Brown Mule brands.

The cook is said to have coined the name "brain food" for cigarettes. The cook noted once that everytime a problem arose, it was almost always customary to take the fixings out of his shirt pocket, roll his cigarette, and enjoy it while he thought out the problem. Coosie also claimed that the reason most all cowboys had a cigarette first thing in the morning was to get their dead brains started, so they could dress.

As part of his usual nightly routine, he would wash the dishes, mix sourdough, grind the coffee beans for the next day, clean and set the beans to soak, and make one last pot of coffee for the nighthawk and night guards. Those denizens of the nocturnal world really did appreciate the hot coffee to warm them up when coming off their watches.

The cook also checked the woodpile and water barrel. This was an opportune time to do these chores, because coosie had at his disposal most all of the cowboys for the evening. The cook was a master at "twisting arms" to get things done. He encouraged, bribed, threatened, and forced the 'pokes to assist him in his time of need...or else. The cook was the absolute ruler of the campsite around the chuck-wagon. Even the ramrod would ask for permission to help himself to a cup of coffee.

The chuck wagon was home to all--the center of their daily activities. Much more than eating went on around the chuck wagon. Coosie's camp was the social gathering place for the hands, and their day-to-day welfare pretty much depended on him. Most cowhands would sit by the chuck wagon, roll a Bull Durham cigarette, and smoke in slumped exhaustion from the taxing day behind them and in anticipation of more of the same on the following day.

After supper, the cowboys gathered around the campfire, and it was a time to pass the remaining hours of the evening by talking over the happenings of the day, resting, playing cards, spinning a few "windys" (tall tales), and singing songs which probably kept all the coyotes away. Perhaps someone would play his harmonica. Contrary to modern movie versions, the guitar or fiddle were not very often found on the trail. Few cowboys actually owned one, and those who did, left it behind as there wasn't much spare room in the chuck wagon to carry it around without being broken.

Before very much later, it was time to drift into their bedrolls, for tomorrow would be another long, hard day. The cook was always the first man to "undress up" and hit the sack, a custom which the rest of the outfit found peculiar. Why was he always so beat? Of course, they never rationalized that the cook had already been up several hours before they even woke up in the morning. Actually, after working hard all day, most all of the hands "went to bed with the chickens," and very shortly after dark, snores could be heard from all.

"Undressing up" was the cowboy's customary method of getting ready for the bedroll. In sequence, the cowboy would take off his boots, socks, and trousers and then sit down on his bedroll, feet under the covers if it was cold. He would reach into his shirt pocket and take out his Bull Durham and cigarette papers and roll his last cigarette of the day, smoking it as he pondered the next day's work to be done. Having finished his smoke, he would take off his jacket, shirt, and finally his hat, and slip into the confines of the bed roll and the accompanying dream land.

Throughout the years, the cook came to be known by a variety of names, some not fit to print or to say to his face. Some of those fit to print here were: bean master, biscuit shooter, coosie, cook, cornbread, pot rustler, dough puncher and grub slinger just to name a few.

Regardless of what events had transpired that day, the cook would always fill a lantern with kerosene and hang it on the camp pole to guide the night-hawk and the men coming in from their turn at night guard. He would also face the tongue of the chuck wagon to the north, using the north star as his guide. This was done to assist the trail boss in the morning in heading the herd in the right direction. Then and only then, was the day's work for coosie finished.

Part 4

MOVING AND SETTING UP CAMP

The job descriptions of the cook were many and varied and were not all directly associated with feeding the hungry cowboys. He usually had the help of a down-an'-out old cowboy who drove the hoodlum wagon in which odds-an'-ends were transported which didn't fit in the chuck wagon. The cook also had the help, to some extent, of the two wranglers, who were usually an older experienced man and a young, strong boy who tended the outfit's horses, *remuda*. Between all of them, the necessary work required to feed the hands was accomplished, sometimes in a harmonious way and other times in a "best we can do" method. While these men worked together as a team, all members acknowledged that it was the cook who called the shots in getting the work accomplished. They were assistants and helpers, but coosie made the decisions.

Often the cook would be assigned a young boy who was too young to do the cowboy'n but old enough to take on some responsibility. "Little Mary" as these young boys were called would be a go-fer this and go-fer that. Contrary to many old-time stories, this was not on-the-job training for the young boy to someday grow up and be a cook. He was only there on a temporary basis, and his ambition was to pay his dues and someday be a working cowboy. Young boys flocked from the East, many of them runaways seeking adventure, drawn by the romantic and dashing image of cowboy life as it was portrayed in the dime novels and big-city newspapers. They hadn't a clue as to the real rigors of cowboy life on the trail. For them, working with coosie served as an apprenticeship, not for cooking, but for Western life. It gave them an opportunity to observe and learn and decide if they wished to pursue the dream that had lured them to the range. Some stayed; most didn't. The ones who did would have to be cowboys for what seemed an eternity before being put out to pasture as a cook. Coosie was their mentor, their teacher, their surrogate mother, but never their role model.

The cook's regimented day-to-day routine necessitated his getting up hours before breakfast. In the morning, he would reverse the "dressing up" process and "dress down." He would first put on his hat, then his shirt and jacket, if it was cold, then reach into his shirt pocket and take out his Bull Durham and cigarette papers and roll the first of his many smokes of the day. This gave him a few minutes in which to get the blood circulating from body to brain. After a few draws of smoke, he stood up, cigarette in mouth, and slipped into his trousers, socks, and finally his boots. He had now dressed down and was ready to begin the day's work. The cook began this ritual while the rest of the hands still dreamed the night away. He usually awoke at three in the morning to get the fires going and rustle up morning chuck for the often unruly and, as he believed, unappreciative hands.

After a hearty breakfast, it was necessary to break up camp, hitch the teams, and load the wagons. The cook almost never did any manual labor not directly associated with cooking. He was, after all, higher in stature in comparison with the other 'pokes. The wrangler and his helper, the night hawk, would harness the four or six mules needed to pull the heavy wagon. They would also hitch up the hoodlum's wagon and help load the wagons.

Time was imperative, as they had to get on the trail and drive the wagons and herd the *remuda* to the next camp site. With the smoke-blackened Dutch ovens and coffee pot hanging on the sides of the wagon, clanging like bells in a church steeple, up into the high seat the cook would climb, and they'd be off to the next camp site. Coosie sure put a lot of bumpy miles on that wagon seat. When any of the cowboys would complain about being stiff or sore from the saddle, Coosie would point out where his bottom had worn the paint off the hard, wooden wagon seat and sanded it smooth, and tell them he had "nary an ounce of pity" for them.

It was when they arrived at the noontime camp site that the night-hawk, finally having been relieved of his responsibilities, picked a spot, unrolled his bed roll, usually near the wagon, and took his allotment of sleep. He would have to be up and at 'em again in a matter of hours to break up camp once more and move on to the evening camp site. After the setting up process was repeated, the night hawk would once again catch a few winks before going on duty.

The cowboys were responsible for rolling up their bedroll with their belongings inside, fastening them in a secure manner, and having them at a designated spot, ready for Coosie and his crew to load.

It was a constant battle with some of the cowboys to get them to correctly roll and tie their bedrolls and leave them properly ready when camp moved. Coosie would get very frustrated to pick up a bed roll to toss on board the wagon and have the improperly-tied bed roll break open and have the contents spread all over the ground. "I wasn't hired to wet nurse these gull-darned idiots."

When this happened, the cook would usually drive off and leave the bedroll there, only informing the owner a few miles down the trail. It didn't take but a couple of cowboys having to back-track to go pick up their gear to indoctrinate the rest of the cowboys to tie their gear more carefully.

If the cowboy was careless a second time, the cook would usually tie the canvas and soogans (blankets) to the back of the wagon and drag them to bits. The cook's measures were guaranteed to make the cowboys' housekeeping manners more in line to his liking.

The cook's rolling kitchen and the hoodlum's wagon followed the pilot rider who knew the country 'round about "like the back of his hand." Behind the chuck wagon followed the wranglers with the *remuda* of up to a hundred and fifty horses. It was always a struggle to stay miles ahead of the main herd of cattle, as they had to get up the trail some ten miles to a designated spot and set up the camp and prepare the noon meal. Once more, they would pack up all the gear and move on to the place selected for the bedding down of the cattle and men for the night and for the evening meal.

The chuck wagon always stayed up front where it would be away from the dust kicked up by the *remuda* of horses. It was imperative that the food source be as clean and free of the dirt and grime associated with the stock as possible. And besides, the cook, used to getting his way, didn't see why he should have to eat all that dust kicked up by the *remuda*.

The trail boss, having selected the camp site, would instruct the cook to set up his camp up-stream from where the cattle would be brought in to drink water. This assured a clean supply of water for cooking and for the cowboys to utilize. One cook had mistakenly set up his camp downstream and, needless to say, the cattle made a muddy mess of the stream. "The water was so muddy and thick, it looked like *frijoles* had been stewing in it," reported one cowboy.

Upon arriving at the camp site, the cook would always turn the front of the wagon to face into the wind, so as to get some kind of protection from the wagon and chuck box for his camp fire. This position also assured that most of the fire pit smoke was blown away from the work area under the shade tent and chuck-box work table. When pressed for time, the shade "fly" as it was known would not be set up. Having to drive the stakes and poles would take away valuable time from the cook's main function. When the camp was going to remain for a day or more, then coosie would set up the fly.

Once his wagon was in position, the cook would call to the wrangler, who had been managing the *remuda,* to unhitch the team and turn them in with the rest of the horses and mules in the *remuda.* The wrangler's responsibility was also to tend to the wood gathering for the cook's fires. Along the trail, the wranglers would constantly be on the lookout for supplies of wood and would throw the wood into the hoodlum's wagon or in the *cuna* tarp under the chuck wagon. It was imperative that the wood supply be ample. The rest of the cowboys would always bring in wood as well and be rewarded by the cook with extra sweets. One of the best ways to stay on the good side of the cook was to keep him supplied with plenty of fire wood.

The next chore for the cook and the hoodlum would then be to unload all the bed rolls and open up the rear box lid, raise the protective fly, and dig a fire pit. The fire irons, metal rods with a point at one end and an eye at the other, would be hammered into the ground at either side of the pit, and the main iron bar some six feet in length was positioned across the pit, suspended through the "eyes" of the end supporting stakes. The firewood was chopped to size if necessary and positioned in the fire pit and the fire started. While the fire heated up, and the necessary hot coals were produced for the Dutch ovens, the cook would begin preparations to cook the food.

The first item to be hung on one of several iron S-hooks suspended on the long bar was the ever-present large (usually holding three to five gallons) pot of coffee. The coffee pot had to always be ready and hot, around the clock, for any and all of the cowboys who happened to be around at any given time of night or day. It was customary for a cowboy to place the coffee pot back where it belonged on the fire to keep it hot for the next man. The stew pots and kettles were also hung from the other hooks.

The camp was now set up, and it was time to cook the meal for the hungry cowboys who would be arriving right on schedule. He had to have the food ready when they rode in, so he tried to adhere to the policy...not a minute early, not a minute late...because their time and his was valuable.

The cycle repeated itself every day, and it was a welcome sight to find out that the camp was going to stay in one spot for a day or so while the stock rested and grazed or the cowboys did their "cowboy'n." It gave the cook a break from having to be constantly on the go. Now he had the time to get re-organized and settle down a bit and catch his breath...kick back a little bit.

It was at these breaks from the constant moving that the cook would really shine. He would take the opportunity to prepare leisurely meals with great pride. This was the time to bake his famous pies and cobblers, for he had the time necessary to do an especially good job. Why, he would even ornament the pie crusts with the outfit's brand.

Repairs to the equipment and wagon could also be done at this time. It is notable to find how many cowboys would be around offering to help the cook at those chores. It was a time to play up to the cook, to get on his good side, to let by-gones be by-gones--at least for the time being. The fact that there was usually a delectable, inviting aroma permeating the camp area made it imperative to be around, in case the cook should need someone's opinion on the cooking of the sweets.

On the other hand, when the camp had to be moved every day, twice a day, these same cowboys seemed to be very busy elsewhere, very apologetic, with lots of remorse at not being able to be there to help out.

A good cook had steadfast rules governing his domain, and they were not negotiable. There was an "understanding" around the camp that no cowboy could ride his horse on the windward side of the camp. This practice helped assure that no trash or dirt would be stirred up and blown into the food being cooked.

No cowboy was permitted to come close to the food containers wearing the "batwing" chaps, as those chaps tended to get into everything. Never would a cowboy step over the open pots which were lined up on the ground. He always stayed on the downwind side of the pots, so as not to stir up any dust to get into the food. He also served himself from that same downwind side. Oh, and one last thing he never did: never take the lids off or peek into the Dutch ovens. Only the cook would take the lids off when ready to serve the chuck.

Pity any cowboy who would dare break these unwritten rules. Any cowboy who was foolish or unfortunate enough to do so was lucky to get off with just a tongue lashing instead of having a frying pan or rolling pin wrapped around his head. A second infraction was met with much tougher ramifications.

The cook reigned supreme, and woe onto the cowboy who dared to infiltrate the cook's sphere or take undue liberties while in the imaginary sixty-foot radius around the chuck wagon.

Probably the most hands-off area was the chuck box itself. All those drawers held the best of the best...sweets, the medicinal liquor, dried fruit, and other items craved by the cowboys. The cook knew this and demanded that no one even think of touching the chuck box lest he be willing to pay the consequences.

It didn't take very long for the novice cowboy to learn that the area around the wagon was the cook's sacred and hallowed terrain. No one, not even the trail boss would dare interfere with the cook's undisputed authority within those perimeters. The cook was master of this small kingdom, guarding it jealously from any encroachments. Then there were those few who would tease the cook and see how far they could penetrate his domain, his private territory, only to be set in their place by the ever-alert cook.

The cook was always trying to make his dominion around the wagon larger. The area he ruled was usually an imaginary circle some sixty feet in diameter around his chuck wagon. But of course, he was always trying to make that circle larger...the larger the circle, the more power he commanded. For after all, isn't a man's wealth judged by the amount of land he controls? Of all the men on the trail outfit, only the cook commanded a piece of ground as he pleased.

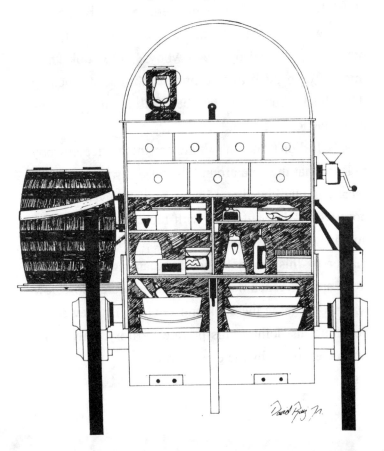

Part 5

COOKING THE MEAL

The Cook had an array of tools and other items necessary to carry out his trade. For the cooking part, he required: numerous pots and pans, large kettles, skillets, several Dutch ovens of various sizes, and of course, the big black coffee pot; essential were long forks and spoons to reach over the hot coals and into the cooking utensils, some butcher knives, and various measuring utensils; a couple of large dish pans, one doubling as a bread pan, and the other, called the camp kettle, used to wash dishes. The pot-hook and a shovel for digging the fire pit and manipulating the white-hot coals were indispensable. The eating and serving utensils were usually battered and overused tin plates, cups, and bowls, and of course the "eating irons:" forks, spoons, and knives.

The cowboys did as they best could, and the cook generally worried more about the cooking of the meal and not so much the serving of it to the uncouth cowboys. Most of them ate with their fingers anyway, instead of using a spoon or fork. As one cowboy quipped, "Hell, if God hadn't intended me to use my fingers, he'd a put prongs at the ends of my hands!"

After digging the fire pit, setting up his pot-rack (which consisted of the two end metal stakes with the six-foot iron bar placed across the top as previously described), and lighting the wood, the cook would begin preparations to cook the food, while the fire heated up which would produce the necessary hot coals for the Dutch ovens.

He would first fill the large coffee pot with water and set it on the fire--the huge coffee pot was the first item to go on the fire, and usually the last item to come off when breaking up the camp. The unmistakable aroma of boiling coffee, blending with the smoke from the fire which filled the surrounding air, always signaled the cook was on duty. He also set a large kettle of water to boil to be used for cooking, washing utensils, washing hands, and for general cleanup. The cook would now get his pot-hook and lift the cast-iron, heavy Dutch oven lids and position them on the fire to heat up. On top of the lids, he would place the three-legged Dutch ovens to start heating up as well. He would then turn his attention to preparing the dough for the bread portion of the meal.

Making the sourdough "starter" was an art which took a considerable amount of devoted attention. Ranch cooks would hoard their starter recipes the way fine chefs guard a recipe for some gourmet dish. The starter was prepared by making a medium-thick starter batter. The cook would take one-half cup of warm water and some hard-wheat flour, and work it well into a wet, sticky dough ball. This was the basic recipe for sourdough starter. To this mixture, coosie added the touches of originality that he chose. He then placed this dough in a bowl, covered it with a damp dish towel held in place with a string, and placed it in a warm area for three days. The natural air around held enough good yeast and bacteria to begin the fermentation process. As soon as the dough began to swell and gave off a yeasty smell, it was ready for use.

The cook would now take a large pan and begin mixing the dough for the bread and biscuits, adding some of the fermented sourdough mixture to the flour, salt, soda, and lard or warm grease. He would knead and twist the bubbling white dough to just the right consistency and then set it aside to "rise."

Every so often, when the sourdough was down to about two cups, the cook would add equal amounts of flour and water to replenish the starter. An ample supply of the starter could thus be kept at the ready for weeks at a time. Some cooks preferred to replenish these equal amounts everytime they took some out, to keep the same amount in the jar.

The main course was then started, usually cuts of meat taken from the side of beef which had been kept deep in the confines of the shaded wagon bed under the bed rolls to keep out the daytime heat. The meat would actually keep very well for up to a week at a time without spoiling, especially after it had "aged" somewhat and had formed a hard, glazed coating on the outside. The secret was to hang out the side of beef to catch the night's coolness and lower its temperature before wrapping it in several layers of canvas and a waterproof slicker the following morning.

It should be taken into consideration that with a hard-working crew of hungry meat-eaters to feed, the butchered beef usually did not last long enough to spoil anyway. When near a farmer's homestead, the trail boss would often take them a side of the forequarters, which the cowboys least desired anyway, preferring the better cuts from the hind quarters. It was a good way to trade for vegetables, eggs, or whatever the nester had an excess of, besides keeping good relations for the next trip through the area.

The meat would be sliced up for cooking in the large Dutch ovens, into which an ample supply of grease had been placed. The oven was placed on top of the hot coals and covered with the hot lid upon which was placed a heap of white-hot coals. While this slowly cooked, the cook would proceed to the next item of business, the potatoes.

Potatoes were a staple food and could be cooked in many different ways, always trying to stay one step ahead of the cowboys and not letting them get tired of the same old potatoes every day. Whatever the method, the potatoes were prepared and set on the fire to cook. The preferred method was to slice them, season them with lots of salt and pepper, and with a flavorful coating of grease, cook them slowly over the fire in one of the large Dutch ovens or skillets.

Actually, because they knew that the potatoes wouldn't keep that long on the trail, the hands weren't too vocal in their objections to coosie cooking them every day. Besides, potatoes were versatile and filling, so it was always customary to stock up on them at towns or farms along the way.

All along, the pot of *frijoles* was cooking and almost ready to serve. With constant moving from camp site to camp site, since beans took several hours to cook, it was an art for the cook to keep a supply of cooked beans ready at all times. Coosie got around this by, after supper, cleaning the beans of any pebbles and foreign objects and placing them in a pot of water to soak overnight to soften them. Soaking the beans would reduce the amount of time needed to cook them.

In the morning, the beans were placed on the fire to simmer as soon as the cook got the fire going. The beans cooked until coosie broke up camp. The hot pot of beans would then be covered and hung from a special hook inside the wagon, protected from the elements. The beans would keep on cooking from the heat retained by the heavy cast-iron pot as the bean pot swung around ever so gently (and sometimes not so gently) with the constant motion of the wagon.

As soon as they set up camp again, and the fire was started, coosie took the bean pot and hung it on one of the hooks to finish cooking. This process was started over every evening, as beans were a staple of trail grub and a favorite with the hands. Anyway, the cook had a lot of pride in his beans; each had his own recipe of added spices, onions, or whatever, which made *his* beans special.

The cook then went back to the final preparation of his biscuits, which had now risen to perfection. He molded the dough into biscuits and placed them into the grease at the bottom of the Dutch oven and turned them over, positioning them side by side with each touching the other slightly. He then placed the pre-heated lid on top of the Dutch oven and shoveled hot coals on top of the lid. It didn't take but a few minutes for the biscuits to turn golden brown, and the food was ready to be served.

Last, but not least, came the dessert: cobblers, pies, puddings, and sweet breads. They were all prepared using the basic biscuit dough to which an ample supply of sugar had been added. Cinnamon sugar was then usually sprinkled on top of the desserts as they baked inside the Dutch oven.

It was quite an art for the cook to be able to manipulate all the variables and still be able to prepare three main meals a day, while moving camp twice. A good cook could accomplish this without a hitch and still come up with on-time, stick-to-your ribs meals for the hungry cowboys. Sometimes, when time didn't permit, the noon meal--dinner--would be "potluck," made up of leftovers or whatever he could rustle up.

The hands, though not entirely happy at not having a full noon meal, understood, as long as it didn't happen too often, especially when it was cold, and a substantial, hot meal sure went a long way in warming up the stomach, as well as the heart.

On the other hand, it was a crying shame what a not-so-talented, disorganized, undedicated cook could do to the groceries, not to mention the outfit's morale.

If, for whatever reason, the cowboys rode into camp ready for their meal, and the food was not ready on time, no one would dare ask, "When will the food be ready?" It was an unpardonable sin to ask the cook what was for dinner or to lift a pot lid to check the ingredients. The cowboys waited as patiently as they could stand to be, quite meekly to say the least, with their faces literally dragging in anticipation.

Finally those most-welcomed words would ring out, along with the most-beautiful sounds of the dinner bell filling the area, "Chuck! Come and git it before I give it to the coyotes!" Or it might be, "Grub p-i-l-e!"

Some cooks would pick up two Dutch oven lids and rub them together, which produced a sound guaranteed to wake up the dead. This method and the infamous triangular-shaped dinner "bell" were not used as much on the trail when the cattle were close by due to the fact that the loud sound could startle the cattle into a stampede.

The men scrambled to get their plate, knife, fork, spoon, and cup from the chuck box and lined up to be served. There were no tables or chairs on the trail. It was customary and the cowboys were used to squatting down on the ground or sitting down with their feet crossed Turkish fashion. The dexterity of the cowboys was a sight to behold...to see them balancing their utensils, sit down while crossing their legs, and then stand back up when finished, all in one easy, graceful motion. And this was accomplished even though the cowboys wore spurs. "Never spilled a drop," claimed one tin-horn visitor from the East, amazed.

No one dared use the cook's chuck wagon fold-down table lid as an eating place. Only the cook and the trail boss enjoyed that privilege, and even they didn't use it that much, for it was the cook's sacred workspace and was cluttered most of the time anyway.

The cook had steadfast rules regarding the cowboy serving himself: he always had to eat what was on his plate, always served himself only what he could eat, and always left enough in the pot for the next man...no seconds until all were assured of a serving. Afterwards, the cowboy would scrape off his plate and place it in the big dishpan full of water that had been placed under the chuck-box lid. The cook's best vocabulary, full of choice adjectives and metaphors, came to light if anyone ever left dishes on the chuck lid or any other place besides the dishpan.

On the other hand, the cowboys didn't really understand nor were they disturbed over the fact that the life of a cook was not necessarily the easiest thing in the world, and they didn't make it any easier. Obstacles were many and occurred with great regularity, and having to put up with the unappreciative and unruly bunch, as coosie perceived the trail hands to be, didn't make it any better. It was a case of coosie constantly being on his toes for fear of cowboys' practical pranks and jokes.

It is easy to understand how a few years of having to put up with these rigors would turn any amiable man into an ill-thinking and bad-tempered tyrant. Why should the cook care about the cowboys? After all, they didn't seem to care about him...until meal time, when everyone lined up for chuck, and then it was always kind and complimentary words. The cook had throughout the years developed, rightfully so, a Dr. Jekyll and Mr. Hyde personality.

The most difficult meal to prepare was the very early breakfast which had to be ready at the first signs of daybreak. In the northern territory because of the high latitudes, the sun usually didn't set until about ten at night, and daybreak came very early in the spring and summer, usually around three or four in the morning. Being that the outfit worked as long as there was daylight, this made for a very long day.

The night hawk, coming in off his watch in the cold grayness of the early morning, would tiptoe among the silent sleepers, wake the cook, and head for the coffee pot. The cook always appreciated his personal "alarm clock."

After coosie had the meal ready to be served, in a loud voice, clear and crisp as a bugle, he would holler for all to hear: "R-o-l-l o-u-t, R-o-l-l o-u-t, you buzzards, while she's hot." Coosie was considerate with the cowpokes, but if they didn't get up right away and head for the chuck wagon, he could be quite grouchy. "Damn your souls, get up!" He would often threaten to throw the food away. Either way, the unmistakable voice heralded the anticipated good breakfast, but also--another hard, demanding day of working the herd.

The hands, with great haste, would jump out of their bedrolls, throw their clothes on, and take a direct bead to the chuck line. A hard and physically-grueling day lay ahead, and they needed all the energy they could muster to get them going. Knowing this, the cook would always put in extra effort and took pride in serving a hearty, if not always scrumptious, breakfast. It was his curtain call...his time to be on center stage.

The menu was usually a generous helping of beef-fried steak or bacon...and they weren't slices, but more like slabs, the greasier the better--it needed to stick to their ribs. Hot biscuits with molasses abounded, and plenty of thick, black coffee; the hands drank copious quantities of the strong brew. No milk in their coffee; heaven forbid anyone would be caught putting "cow lick" into their mugs. Sugar was fine, as they were always craving sweets in any way, shape, or form. Sometimes, if time permitted, coosie would surprise the hands with stacks of griddle-cakes.

Considering the trials and tribulations found on the trail, coosie and the cowboys had one common ground on which they could agree: FOOD. Most full-time cooks derived great satisfaction in preparing delectable, aromatic meals, and they were good at it, or they didn't last long. The hands derived great satisfaction in eating that food, and they too were good at eating, so it was a mutually-beneficial, if unequal, partnership.

Part 6

HUMOR AROUND THE CHUCK WAGON

Being away from society and having free time on their hands after their work was done for the day, the cowboys often would carry out their pranks. All the hands liked a good joke on someone, as long as it wasn't on themselves, but on the other fellow. The cowboy's youthful, vigorous good health and disposition filled him with a natural tendency toward humor and play, and his release came in the rough-an'-ready practical jokes, tricks, and pranks prevalently found around the cow camp, and more often than not, around the chuck wagon.

The wit and humor was very much a part of the outfit, getting the cowboys through trying times and situations; sometimes it was just for the fun of it.

The pranks were occasionally a spontaneous reaction to on-the-spot situations, but more often than not, the joshing was elaborately planned. The cowboy led a very dangerous and lonely life, and this probably was the reason he cherished hospitality, laughter, and friendship all the more. Humor was the perfect way to achieve that companionship.

A smart trail boss would control the situation as best he could and would often hire a known young jokester just to keep the camp camaraderie in gear and the cowboys happy. It kept them in anticipation waiting to see what shenanigans they could pull on each other.

Not being prudent by nature, the prank specialist was mighty fast to give his sense of humor free rein, which resulted in his capers likely being plenty rough, robust, and reckless, a reflection of the kind of life he lived. By common nature, the prankster was a reckless, don't-give-a damn fool who hadn't caution enough at that particular moment to fear the consequences. He would deal with that later if he had to.

Usually these pranks, no matter how vicious, would never result in a fist fight, for all this rough play was given and taken in good faith and was a part of life around the camp. It was uncommon for a cowboy to lose his temper over a joke; he rather just waited for the opportunity and circumstances to be ripe, and then he would get even.

To completely lose his composure and not take it in stride was an open invitation to the others, and he would be put to further and even rougher tests; teasing could get pretty intense. Kind of like the wild bronc'--the more he bucks and fights, the more he will be ridden, until he is broken and falls in line as anticipated.

A usual target of those pranks was the cook who would himself retaliate at an opportune time. Many humorous incidents occurred throughout the years, some with happy endings and some with disastrous results. The telling of tall tales also became a part of the cook's province, and the cowboys were expected to extend the courtesy of pretending to believe him.

Cowboys were and still are natural-born storytellers, especially after a long day of punching cattle, when sitting at night before a blazing campfire near the chuck wagon. Old timers still narrate tales and yarns, or "windies," as they were known, all trying to outdo each other, recounting some of these humorous events. A large percentage of the tales seemingly had to do with the trail cook who was on both the giving and receiving end.

One evening, coosie gave what was probably his best "windy" performance to a crew of mostly greenhorn and gullible 'pokes who happened to be around the fire after supper: "Once we were out where there was scant fire-wood pickings, and I had to get the meal ready," said coosie, with a convincingly serious look on his face. "Boy, was I in a bind! I was as worried as a frog in the desert!"

The cook, having caught the hands' attention went on to tell them how he had set up his coffee pot and Dutch ovens filled with meat and bread on the prairie grass and set fire to the grass. "Damn northern wind came up, and I had to constantly move the pots and pans to keep them over the flames...kept me pretty busy." Glancing over at the trail boss and winking his eye, the cook went on, never missing a beat. "By the time the food was ready to serve the hungry hands, I realized I was five miles from camp."

The cook would control the most unruly of the cowboys with a simple threat of not cooking a dessert. The rest of the cowboys would usually get the unruly cowboy back in line lest they all suffer the wrath of the cook's authority. He was also known on occasion to put some salt or sugar and sometimes a lizard or horned toad in certain bedrolls or boots. One of the most severe pay-backs was simply to make up a pot of "belly wash," weak coffee...lordy, did that get the hands' attention, for it was a penance to drink coffee not heavy and black enough to suspend a horseshoe, as the saying went.

The cook would often get even with the cowboys with his cooking, or lack of cooking. One cook once took out a beauty of a pudding from his camp oven and gave all the smiling cowboys their share. One bite and they all started spitting and cursing up a storm...cookie had loaded the pudding up with salt instead of sugar. With a great big smile on his face, the cook reached down and came up with the real pudding. The laughs were plenty and the cowboys went to bed quite happy. Actually the cook's jokes were appreciated by all, because the cowboys always knew that the cook would make good on his jokes with the real thing. It did keep them on their toes though.

Another favorite story told was of one cowboy in particular who had once before been designated temporary cook because of his insulting remarks. After a difficult stint, he was finally replaced, to the other cowboys' delight, with a newly-found full-time professional cook.

One day, the cowboy in question rode into camp after a hard day's work and sat down to supper. When he took a big spoonful of the beans on his plate, he almost had to spit them out, as they were more than a bit on the salty side. He complained wholeheartedly to the cowboy next to him, "These are the mouth-puckeringest beans I have ever 'et. Coosie was heavy-handed with that salt when he made these, wasn't he?"

Catching himself as he realized the cook had overheard his remark, and noticing the cook's hopeful look, he very quickly amended his comment, "But the extri' salt sure comes in handy on these hot and humid days. Yep...just the way I like 'em!" Needless to say, the cook stood there, apron in hand, tapping his finger-tips on the wagon's work table, ready to pass the apron on. He watched the cowboy "happily" eat all the beans on his plate.

With a smirk on his face, the avenging cook served the reluctant cowboy another plateful of the beans. "Since you enjoyed my beans so much, let me give you another serving...and don't be afraid to ask for all you want," said the cook with his great big pearly whites showing almost from ear to ear. The hesitant cowboy had to eat the second helping or face the consequences.

In a nonchalant manner, the other hands tried mixing the rest of their food into the salty beans, trying to cut back the saltiness. Some mixed in rice, potatoes, or meat, and these helped somewhat, but the real solution came from one of the more innovative hands: "Pass me the lick, Coosie. I do believe I'll have me some "Boston Baked Beans." The rest of the hands hurriedly poured on the molasses and mixed it with the beans and proceeded to wipe off their plates with the rest of the biscuits.

One story worth telling is that of a very industrious cook who, along with the rest of the cowboys, had been invited to attend a dance at a nearby community along the trail. There would be many ladies from the surrounding farms and other small communities in attendance, just waiting for the cowboys to come to the dance.

Most cowboys didn't really bother about how they looked while on the trail, but now they were all lined up for haircuts from the cook, being as nice as they could be.

The cook, having to stay behind 'till he cleaned up the after-supper camp mess and washed the dishes, pots and pans, and put everything away, would miss out on the nicer ladies. The cowboys had been pulling his leg all day about how he had best stay in camp because all the pretty ladies would be taken by the time he finally made it to the dance. But the cook had a plan, and proceeded to carry it out with the utmost precision.

He very patiently fixed a big supper of beef and fried potatoes that let off a most delectable aroma around the camp when the Dutch oven lid was opened. The cowboys, who by now had cleaned up somewhat in readying for the dance, dug in and ate their fill. They ate with such haste that no one even noticed that the cook had not eaten...had they noticed, they might have been suspicious.

Upon arriving at the dance, the trail hands weren't faring so well with the ladies, as most only could get one dance before the maiden would politely decline another dance and retreat with a shake of the head. The poor old unsuspecting cowboys were now relegated to one side of the building, wondering why they were being ignored. Had they not cleaned up and even shaved and washed up, put on clean clothes and all? What was going on here? "Surely I'm not *that* ugly," commented one 'poke.

About that time the cook arrived, walked right by the group, and made a beeline for the ladies, and for the rest of the evening was kept on his feet dancing up a storm while the rest of his crew couldn't beg a dance.

The trail boss showed up and went over to find out why the men were all in a group instead of spread out and dancing. No more than a few words had been exchanged when he jumped back a couple of feet. "What in tarnation have you all been eating?" he inquired, holding his nose with one hand and fanning with the other hand as if to ward off the terrible smell. "All of you smell something awful."

The truth finally came out when the cook confessed that knowing he was going to be late to the dance, and fearing all the pretty girls would be spoken for, he had taken action to even out the situation. He had loaded up the potatoes with a generous amount of garlic and had gotten the unsuspecting hungry men smelling like unwanted pole-cats.

So mischief went in all directions, from cowboy to cowboy, from cook to cowboy, and from cowboy to cook. It wasn't only the cowboys who gave the cook headaches--one unsuspecting mule pulled a prank on one cook and is a story still making the campfire circles.

Story has it that there was this hot-tempered cook known as Bullhead Bill who was with the LU outfit up in Montana. There had been an old mule who had been with the chuck wagon for so many years, that when it was finally retired and put out to pasture, would still persist in following the wagon from one range to the other.

That darn mule behaved more like a dog than the long-eared varmint he was. Bullhead Bill had always been fond of the unusually friendly mule and let it hang around. Hell, he actually had some juicy conversations with the mule when there was no one else around to jaw with.

There came a time when several outfits were camped close to each other while on a large roundup. The 79 outfit had a well-known cook named Vinegar Joe who had the distinction of making the best pies in the territory. Could this have been the cook responsible for inventing the much liked "Vinegar Pie" fancied by many? *Quien sabe...*

One day, while a joint, two-outfit, roundup was going on, Vinegar had some spare time after the noon dinner meal was done with and was in the mood to bake some pies. After all the work was finished, he proudly lay out the masterpieces on the chuck lid to cool, and decided to stroll on over to the LU camp and flap some jaw with his *compadre* Bullhead for awhile.

Vinegar's conversation eventually got around to how good his pies were, and how the men would hold him in high regard that evening when he pulled out his prize-winning pies. "When it comes to baking, no one, present company included, can touch my pies!" Vinegar kept on and on, not being one bit shy about spreading the self-praise hot, heavy, and thick.

As they sat there jawing and trying to outdo each other, Bullhead noticed his old mule stride on over and into Vinegar's chuck fly tent. He decided not to say anything and just kept on with the conversation as if nothing was going on.

Vinegar suddenly jumped up and let out an array of cuss words that would sizzle bacon. That old mule had walked up from the direction of the 79 wagon, and as it approached the two cooks, it was obvious that the old mule had pie filling smeared all over its mouth.

Vinegar became more belligerent, and the smiling-faced Bullhead countered in defending his mule *compadre* friend. Vinegar blamed Bullhead for allowing that dumb mule to hang around all the time and allowing it to run uncontrolled, causing havoc all of the time. This incident broke up their long-time friendship, and as long as that mule was around, Vinegar would have nothing to do with Bullheaded Bill. After that, Vinegar Joe would always say, "My pies are ab-so-loot-ly the best! No living critter can resist them." He had gotten the last word in the confrontation.

There was once an incident with a not-so-clean cook who having just finished his noon chores decided to take advantage of a nearby creek. He went over and took off his clothes, except for his hat, hung them on a mesquite bush, jumped in, and was frolicking around like a kid--whooping and hollering all kinds of songs. Unannounced to him, two old dry cows came nosing around and low and behold...salt!

Cattle have a natural need for salt, and it was right there in front of them in the form of dried, salty sweat on the old cook's dirty clothes. Needless to say, they were making a meal of the clothes, and by the time the cook realized what was going on, it was too late. The cows had shredded the clothes to smithereens. He was able to salvage the shirt, but one sleeve was already gone.

Old coosie made a run for the wagon, hoping none of the hands had noticed, but seeing the stark-naked old guy with only his hat on and what was left of the shirt, gave away what had happened. "You should have jumped in with your clothes on, Coosie. They needed it more than you did," yelled one of the hands. The old cook learned a lesson and from that day on was more careful when he hit the creeks.

There was the time the cook had not taken a bath in so long that the hands had a hard time trying to stay up-wind and away from the stench. They finally got together and held a "kangaroo court" right then and there, found the cook guilty, and proceeded to carry out the sentence. The cook violently objected during the unofficial, official proceedings. When the gavel went down, old skunk-scent tried to make a run for it, but the cowboys promptly caught him and carried out the sentence...threw him into the creek, clothes and all.

They all jumped in after him and proceeded to give both man and clothes a soapy reception. The cook, obviously outmanned, finally gave up and accepted the consequences. As they eventually let him go, he gathered his wits and very nicely exited the watery misery, with a smile on his face....

To a man, they looked at each other and realized that they all had best be on their guard, as they were now obviously going to be the recipient of the cook's wrath--if they only knew when? The tale of that cook's revenge is unrecorded, but one can be sure, he ultimately had the last word.

Another funny tale is told about the time a guest from the East came to visit. Now the cook in residence was the one and only well-known cook appropriately named "Crow" for he was the blackest Negro ever to come to these parts. The name was coined by some prankster cowboy no doubt, and the nickname stuck.

One of Crow's most famous dishes was his soft-shelled turtle stew. It was a delicacy very few could taste unless they worked for the same outfit or happened by in transit on the day Crow had prepared his masterpiece. An enterprising cowboy caught one of the biggest turtles ever seen in those parts and proudly brought it in to the cook, knowing full well that the delicious stew would be served the next day. The cook staked the turtle on the river bank where they were camped to hold until the next morning.

The next morning, the visitor, who just happened to be a traveling ventriloquist entertainer, hid in the water, only his head sticking out, behind some bushes growing on the river bank. He was in a position immediately next to the staked turtle and out of sight, his head hidden conveniently with some bushes. When Crow came over to take out the main course for that evening's meal, he took the turtle out of the water and held it by one of its legs while he untied the line with the other hand.

The ventriloquist, in a high pitched voice cried out, "Crow, Crow, what in tarnation are you going to do with me?"

The startled Crow, with eyes big as melons, looked at the turtle, who by now was looking back at him eye-to-eye, and nervously replied, "Suh?"

"Crow, what are you a-going to do with me?"

"I'm a-going to let you go right now tu'tle, suh!" replied the now trembling Crow, which he did and ran off quickly as his legs could carry him.

Needless to say, the outfit, most of whom were in on the prank, laughed for days and days afterwards. The last laugh was on themselves though, because Crow could not be convinced the whole episode had been concocted and carried out as a joke. Crow would never again cook his famous turtle stew.

Many of the humorous stories told about the cooks centered around dishes for which they were famous. For example, one summer roundup time, the chuck wagon was camped on Kennedy Canyon when one wrangler named Broadhammer had been delayed in coming in for supper. Upon arriving, he found out that coosie had cooked his very favorite dish of all...tomato pie. Needless to say, the wrangler was whining and crying about how those dirty bums had eaten all of the pie, leaving almost none for him. He was all out of sorts over the whole thing, and the other hands were quite irritated over his constant bellyaching.

The cook finally agreed to *consider* preparing another delicious tomato pie for Broadhammer. "You can't eat a whole pie by yourself, and the others have already had their fill, or I'd bake one up for you."

"Oh yes I can!" replied Broadhammer, anticipating having a whole tomato pie to himself to enjoy. Besides, he had the reputation of always "padding out his belly," eating everything in sight. He could really pack that food in.

One of the cowboys talked the cook into making up another pie with the assurance that they would all make sure that the wrangler would eat the whole thing. That's all the cook needed to hear. Taking his cue, he agreed to do it, much to everyone's delight.

Now a twelve-inch Dutch oven, using a number three can of Tomatoes, makes a pretty good-sized pie, filling up the pot about three-quarters full. When the pie was ready, Broadhammer began eating as if there was no tomorrow. After three ample servings, he realized that maybe it was a bit too much to consume by himself.

"Here, guys, I'll share with you, knowing how much you like tomato pie," but he had no takers willing to help out. Broadhammer began to sense the cowboys closing in on him, selecting favorable positions, literally cutting off any avenue of escape. He pulled his hat down low over his eyes, as he nervously ate, and glanced very carefully out from under the brim, looking for an escape route. Suddenly he threw his plate aside and began to run, but he was subdued before he even got ten yards away.

The cowboys dragged him back and, much to coosie's delight, proceeded to force-feed the rest of the pie to Broadhammer. Stories around the campfires say that Broadhammer couldn't ever see another tomato pie without turning blue to the gills. Everyone had a real good laugh and coosie never ever got any more demands from any of the hands requesting personal dishes.

Other pranks took place within the circle of the chuck cook's domain which were usually targeted at greenhorn cowboys. One favorite prank was to turn the saddle around and remount it backwards on the greenhorn's horse. A visiting victim who had arrived at the ranch in a buggy would come out to leave and find his buggy and horses intact, except that the horse was on one side of the fence and the buggy was on the other side of the fence.

The cook was always "helpful" to the new greenhorn cowboys in camp, often "hinting" at what they should do to so-'n-so. Old coosie had a lot of his retaliations taken care of indirectly by these unsuspecting young greenhorns who willfully and expeditiously did as "advised" to get on the good side of the cook.

Thus coosie was quite a chameleon of a character, with many personalities to his credit. He would change colors as best suited him at any given time. Deep inside, he had that streak of humor found in all cowboys of the time, which kept everyone on their toes and in good spirits. Day-to-day life on the trail was difficult enough, but the bond of laughter which existed among the hands went a long way in maintaining their spirits.

Part 7

WHAT COOSIE SERVED THE COWBOYS

Food constituted the greater part of the boss's expense account for the trail drive. It took large amounts of food to feed the twenty or thirty cowhands three times a day.

Hominy, rice, J. Lusk peaches, potatoes, music roots (sweet potatoes), sugar, salt, onions, and, of course, dried fruits were purchased in great quantities, when possible by the barrel. Pinto beans, extra coffee beans, Red X flour, and other food products came in large sacks weighing fifty to one hundred pounds each. Large cans, in sizes varying from one to five gallons each in size, containing lard, baking powder, Caddy Black tea, coffee, milk, vegetables, corn starch, and other similar items were also necessary. Tins of spices such as cayenne pepper, cinnamon, and nutmeg and bottles of vanilla and lemon extracts, and vinegar were staple items in the chuck wagon larder.

In cases (which occurred quite frequently) where the cook was of Mexican descent, he would also carry along, in addition to the above standard staples, other items inspired by his Mexican influence. He loaded up with bold and exciting seasonings of chilies, comino seeds, garlic, coriander, oregano, and various others. The blending of these spices was a culinary secret sometimes handed down from generation to generation.

Mmm, mmm, what a cook could do with the little he had to work with while out on the trail. He could cook a meal of hot steaks freshly cut off the hindquarter and fried in lots of fat. The cook would toss some flour into the left-over hot grease, let it brown up good, and serve the tasty gravy, sometimes called "Texas Butter," with the sourdough biscuits or bread.

He would serve baked short ribs or slumgullion stew, fried spuds with onions, or a hot pot of beans with loads of salt pork added. The large but light sourdough or baking powder biscuits fresh out of the Dutch oven complemented the meal. Oh, and then those cobblers, puddings, and pies finished off the rib-sticking meals. If time and circumstances didn't allow for a special dessert, then the bacon drippings mixed with some "lick" (dark molasses), and sopped up with hot biscuits were a favorite. Not all trail cooks could prepare meals like this, but many were experienced and innovative in their food preparation. The cowboys did not tire of the same menu being prepared over and over. They came in hungry from their hard work and appreciated a hot meal that would re-energize them and calm the rumbling in their bellies.

But wait! Lest we forget to mention a steady flow of good old Arbuckle's coffee "strong enough to float a horseshoe" as the saying went. The coffee usually was taken straight out of the pot, thick and black. Some 'pokes would add ample amounts of sugar, as all cowboys seemed to have a bottomless-pit craving for sweets--sweets in any way, shape, or form.

Though the cowboys thrived on coffee, the cook always had tea in the chuck box for the few cowboys who favored it (especially the transplanted Irishmen). The black tea, as well as herbal teas, was also brewed for medicinal purposes for ailing cowboys.

In the cool evenings, after their supper and while visiting around the campfire before "plastering their ear to the pillow", the 'pokes enjoyed a drink inspired by the Mexicans.

Atole was very simple to make with the most basic of readily-available ingredients. It was really a sweet, gravy-type drink cooked in the traditional Mexican way by melting clean, unused lard in a pot, stirring in some flour or meal and some sugar and cinnamon. Water was slowly added and stirred constantly to bring the mixture to the consistency of "runny gravy." The hot *Atole* proved to be a healthful, nourishing, and delicious drink. It had that "stick-to-your-ribs" consistency which all cowboys liked.

Milk was another item altogether and was generally used exclusively for cooking and not for the coffee or for drinking. One of the major reasons for not utilizing milk more was due to the problem of storage and spillage, which presented a major obstacle. Another reason was that fresh milk was troublesome to come by on the trail. One would think that with all those thousands of cattle on the drive, milk would be plentiful. But these were not your tame dairy or farm cows. The simple fact is that trying to milk one of the semi-wild, cantankerous, undomesticated mother cows was next to impossible to accomplish. It was also a job which cowboys spurned. A cowboy would work and struggle with the ornery critters all day and night, cussing them with ear-bending words, but when it came to milking one--well that was another story altogether. He would draw a straight line and refuse. Milking cows was for farmers, women, children, but NOT for a cowhand. Even when canned milk was introduced, "canned cow" as it was called, the cowboy still viewed it with great suspicion. Besides, as one cowboy commented, "Milk gives you the breath of a baby calf...yuk!" It might be assumed, with a little speculation, that if cows produced some sort of spirits, instead of white milk, the cowboys would have solved the problem...pronto!

One industrious cook came up with a way in which a form of butter could be taken along on the trail. He experimented and found that if he boiled the butter and then clarified it by skimming the solids off the top, the resulting oil could be poured into a tin container whose top was then soldered airtight. This procedure allowed the butter to be kept for a long time, retaining its flavor. Sometimes, after a while, the butter became somewhat rancid, but it was still usable.

Though there were various foods available to the cook, most cooks created their own special cuisine from the three "B's" basic staple foods: beef, beans and bread. These were expected to be served at every meal in most any way, shape, or form.

The main course was beef, preferably three times a day. Most of the cowboys were a bit fastidious in their individual tastes, and most preferred steaks from the hindquarters, cooked in various ways, or rib roasts. The less desirable part of the beef, the forequarters, was usually left for last or would be traded to settlers along the way for eggs and vegetables.

Another method of taking meat with them on the trail was to cut the meat into thin flaky strips, salting it, and drying the strips in the sun, producing beef jerky. This made an excellent snack meal, especially for the riders when they had to be gone all day from the camp.

During roundups (which sometimes took months) there were some ranch owners who were so doggoned stingy, they couldn't see slaughtering a beef just to feed the hands. They kept pigs for that and would rather feed their cowboys pork, as long as the cowboys were in the ranch area, to avoid slaughtering cows which could be taken on the trail and sold.

Now, the cook usually did use salt pork for preparing the beans and to season other dishes, and they were great tasting...but to make a complete meal out of pork? That was going too far.

This type of parsimonious attitude on the part of the boss could cause a high turnover. One cowhand who quit such an outfit said he was "fed pork-hide so often and in such quantities that he actually sweated lard, and instead of snoring at night, he was snorting and grunting!" Another hand swore he was even afraid to feel his southern-most end for fear he might discover he had grown a curly tail.

When the cook had ample time during a break in the constant moving around, he would bake pies made out of the dried fruit he stocked in large quantities. The pies were usually made with a traditional double crust, sugar and cinnamon sprinkled on the top crust. Sometimes the cook would shape a strip of dough in the shape of the outfit's brand and position it on top of the pie. Extra touches like that always pleased the cowboys who were sure to comment on them.

The canning industry was still in its infancy at that time. Canned fruits, other than peaches were not too commonly found. People baked and cooked with fresh or with dried fruits. Apple was a favorite fruit of the 'pokes, and they loved the pies made out of them...for a while. After a time, however, the apple pies would become monotonous, and soon these pies would not be so popular after all. Due to lack of availability and higher cost, the other dried fruits would be consumed sooner, as the lesser quantities would be eaten up at a faster rate. Apples, being more readily available, in more abundance, easier to dry, and thus cheaper, lasted an eternity it seemed.

One cowboy coined a poem that indicated the monotony of the dried apple diet:

"I shore don't mean to criticize,
But I'm tired of all those apple pies.
I"ve et them till they bug my eyes,
So don't serve me dried apple pies."

When a cow was butchered out on the range, the industrious camp cook would generally prepare his good-old-standby dish: "Son-of-a-bitch" stew, or "Son-of-a-gun" stew, the toned-down name for it that was used in certain circles when ladies where present. When was this dish invented? The story goes that one day, the economically-minded cook was butchering a cow when he noticed all the "innards," which he was throwing out for the buzzards and coyotes every time a beef was butchered.

Coosie decided to make good use of these up-to-then unused innards, and feed them to his own buzzards, the cowpokes. The main reason those parts had always been discarded was that, unlike the regular meat from the front and rear quarters, those parts would spoil almost immediately.

Coosie reasoned that a cow produced meat which he was obliged to cook. Since these innards were from the cow, they therefore had to be considered meat, no matter how anyone else looked at it, or if they agreed with him or not.

Coosie took the animal's innards: the brain, tongue, sweetbreads, liver, heart, cut tripe which had been carefully washed out, and whatever else he could salvage. Except for the horns, hooves, and hide, he cut almost everything into bite-sized pieces and threw them into the large Dutch oven pot . He added water to cover the whole mess, salt and pepper, a few skunk eggs (onions), and sometimes some *Chile Pequin*. He then simmered the concoction for several hours, till all was tender and cooked to perfection.

The first unsuspecting cowboy to ride into camp that evening for supper served himself a plateful, and took one spoonful into his mouth--just long enough to spit out and reach for his coffee to kill the overpowering taste in his mouth. "Son of a bitch, Coosie!" yelled the cowpoke. "What in hell have you done cooked this time?" Sensing his predicament at possibly being promoted to cook, he continued "Let me have some more...it sure hits the spot!"

The concoction had been inadvertently named right then and there, and the name stuck, even against the wishes of the cook who probably had a better-suited name in mind.

Needless to say, there wasn't any other choice for the meal, so all the cowboys reluctantly served up. The more they ate, the more they began to like it, and before long all the stew was done e'ten. Forget the ingredients...this stew was mouth-watering good.

When properly prepared, this dish was one of the most-desired meals requested by the cowboys. The recipe spread to other camps, carried by the cowboys and cooks moving from one cow camp to another, or from one ranch to another. To this day, Son-of-a-gun stew is still prepared all over the West, though some modern-day cooks have pretty much ruined the real taste by adding potatoes and other vegetables and spices.

The first recorded gourmet dish on the trail was served by an LS Ranch chuck wagon up in the

Texas panhandle. It seems that there was this cowboy named Duncan Hayes on the payroll. Duncan was actually educated and came from a prominent family from Louisiana. In fact, while on the LS payroll, this young man had actually written some articles for the *Louisiana Gazette.* The young Duncan's doctor had dictated that he move to the dry climate out West to improve his health, and that is how he found himself in the great outdoors.

One day while the chuck wagon was camped near a creek, Dunk found a large hole of clear water which was teeming with crayfish. He excitedly caught a mess of them and took them to the cook in anticipation of a great meal for supper.

Coosie was horrified, to say the least. In these parts, people just didn't eat those slimy critters. "You want to eat them things, *you* cook 'em," replied the cook with a definite and unquestionable tone in his voice, probably throwing in a few choice words or phrases from his extensive, expressive collection.

Dunk poured boiling water over the crawdads, then shelled and saved every tail. One look at the nasty mess, and the cook was having second thoughts. "You aren't going to cook those nasty things in one of *my* Dutch ovens are you?"

"They're not nasty," Dunk replied, "and I'll need some lard, rice, tomatoes, and onion, and a few other ingredients to make the sauce." This increased the cook's wrath, but he reluctantly produced the ingredients.

When the hands showed up for supper, Dunk invited them to partake in his culinary effort, stressing the fact that he'd made them with crawfish tails. Their refusal was vigorous and final, to say the least.

Coosie, feeling Dunk had gone to so much trouble preparing the dish, and also noticing everybody was being so rude, accepted the invitation. "The stew probably won't kill me, so I'll accept a bite or two of the dish."

Coosie tasted the mixture and got the surprise of his life! He filled his plate with the delicious stew and sat down next to Dunk, and both proceeded to clean out the whole mess of crawdad stew. They consumed ample amounts of sourdough biscuits to sop up the sauce, which the cook called gravy. But different and unique dishes such as Dunk's creation were generally not welcomed by the cowboys. They wanted "hearty," not gourmet.

One invention which really helped assure the cowboys with a variety of food products was the "airtights" or canned goods as they are known today.

Though canned foods were scarce and not much of a selection could be made, they did make life for the cook somewhat easier. The most common canned foods were fruits and vegetables...especially the tomatoes and peaches which were so desired by the outfit.

A variety of vegetables and fruits sometimes were traded or bought from a farmer along the way. One particular farmer had an unusually large watermelon patch, and the outfit had arrived at just the right time of the season...the 'melons were ripe an' ready for picking. Needless to say, the trail boss and coosie made a trade right then and there for a load of watermelons. They traded a young calf, which was a boon to the farmer, who didn't have much stock to speak of. "This young calf will grow up to be a good milk cow," said the grateful farmer, grinning from ear to ear. As the trail boss drove the wagonload of watermelons away, he glanced back and waved a cheerful farewell to the young farmer who was happily leading the calf away...a fortuitous deal for both parties.

Coosie would put a few melons in the cool streams they camped at and take them out just in time to eat them after their supper. Coosie would take his trusty knife and carve out huge slices for the hands.

He would then put out an empty jar so the hands would deposit their melon seeds, which would then be dried and planted at the proper time of the year back at the main ranch headquarters. Coosie was very industrious.

When a camp was to be in one location for a few days, the cook would get some volunteers to dig a hole some five feet long by three feet wide by four feet deep, although the dimensions could vary. In the early evening, the hands would build a large fire inside the pit and keep it going for a few hours to build up an ample supply of reddish-white, hot coals.

Meanwhile, coosie would quarter one whole side of beef, season it with his favorite spices, wrap it with clean white cloth, and then use an outer wrap around it...usually gunny-sack. The quarters would then be tied with wire. These meat bundles would be positioned on a rack especially made out of four corner steel rods with two side rods resting on them across the width of the pit. Four steel rods would then be laid across these, forming a grid which would hold the meat. The bottom of the meat rack was situated just above the hot coals, and after the meat was in place, the pit would be covered with wooden planks carried especially for this reason. A heavy tarp was then placed over these planks, and a layer of dirt some six or more inches thick was thrown over the tarp to seal in all the heat and prevent any loss of the resulting hot steam to escape.

This meat was left in the pit all night and into the next afternoon, when it was unearthed carefully. "A sight to behold," said one cowboy, smelling the mouth-watering aroma, and then seeing the tender meat cooked to perfection. All the flavors were held in, due to the sealed pit and the cloth wrapping that retained the juices. This was the favorite method of cooking that most all the hands preferred; *barbacoa* the *vaqueros* called it, or Bar-B-Que as the cowboys Americanized it with time.

A gastronomical dish favored by the Mexican vaqueros was a whole beef head, skinned, cleaned, seasoned, wrapped, and cooked slowly in the pit the way a side of beef would be prepared.

Another food product that was often cooked in the pit alongside the meat was beans. An emptied five-gallon lard can (or something similar) would be filled with pre-boiled beans. Before the tight-fitting metal lid was put on, the beans would be loaded with salt pork or a ham bone and some spices. This might be considered the forerunner of the crock pots that are used today. Cooking the beans slowly for a long time in the pit produced a thick-sauced, flavorful dish.

The pits used by the chuck wagon cooks were modified, smaller versions of the elaborate pit areas used at the main ranches. Some of the ranch pits were huge and could hold several sides of beef to feed hundreds of hungry cowboys and guests, especially when dances and celebrations were held.

Whatever else could be said of the open-air camp cooks, good or bad, it all came down to one indisputable fact: they were, first and foremost, excellent meat cooks. They were proud of their meat concoctions, and didn't do such a bad job of the bread and biscuits either.

Part 8

DR. *COCINERO* AND COWBOY MEDICINE

Generally being far from most any sign of civilization and certainly from a doctor or dentist, much less a hospital...well it was a touchy situation. The outfits had to do their own doctoring with whatever little practical knowledge they had picked up through the years and with what they learned from one another. In real critical cases of sickness or accidents, the patient would be put on a wagon and hauled to the nearest town that had a doctor. Sometimes the trip could take days, and the poor old chap hung on as best he could. His only other option was to be treated by coosie, who was the appointed trail medical specialist.

Whereas he liked having a small town with a doctor in residence close by, coosie hated to see the 'pokes go into town for some fun. Visits to town meant cowboys returning the next day with all kinds of cuts and bruises and hangovers. Treating them would take him away from his regular duties.

Coosie was usually one of the older cowboys and had been around for a long time. Knowing and having seen just about every ailment to be found on the trail pretty much made him the designated doctor, dentist, pharmacist, and psychologist of the outfit...not to mention being part-time veterinarian, peacemaker, and the holder of countless other titles.

Dr. Coosie carried very few medicines or so-called medicines, as he really didn't need many to cure a sick-feeling, down-and-out cowboy real quickly. In his wagon was the primary "medicine" he usually could count on: his can of Black Draught, a repelling, nauseous potion guaranteed to cure almost any ailment. It was the accepted belief that the worse the smell and taste of any medicine, the surer the cure would be. Judged by these standards, Black Draught was outstanding.

If this potion didn't work, then old coosie would resort to his standby stock of so-called prescriptions. The bottle of turpentine, which had medicinal purposes for what ailed the cowboy on the outside as well as what ailed him on the inside, was a tried and proven medicine. If there wasn't any turpentine, then the kerosene from the lantern would do. Kerosene had excellent coagulant properties when applied to open wounds.

Horse liniment was so stout that the receiver of the treatment felt the hot liniment more than he felt whatever ailed him at the time. Liniments made from turpentine, mustard seed, and wintergreen oil treated muscle pain. Hot and cold poultices were commonly used for a number of maladies. Coosie also carried along some quinine, and some kind of laxative such as cod-liver oil or castor oil--the hands didn't like the way coosie always seemed to prescribe "a good laxative" for almost any disease.

Needless to say, this is the reason cowboys were such a rough and durable bunch, for they had learned how to cure themselves as best they could without having to resort to going to the cook for treatment. This was especially true if the ailing cowboy had recently pulled a prank on the cook and was in line for retaliation. Sometimes an injured cowboy would actually have to be coaxed and man-handled into going to Dr. Coosie.

Broken bones were frequent occurrences, and all the cook could do was set the bone as best he could and wrap it up and take out the medicinal bottle of bourbon. This bottle was kept only for serious complications like broken bones or dental work. It is doubtful if any cowboy would trade a broken bone for the right to have a few shots of bourbon, but as long as he already had the broken bone....

There was a certain amount of "self doctoring" going on all the time. One remedy for a bad cavity with its accompanying pain was to saturate a small piece of cotton with oil of cloves, stuff it into the cavity, and bite hard 'till the nerve deadened somewhat. We know now that this remedy worked because of the eugenol contained in the clove oil. Another toothache remedy was to peel off some of the soft inside tissue found in the little knots on the horse's legs, just above the knees. This soft tissue, known as the chestnut, would be rolled up into a little ball and stuffed into the tooth cavity to keep the air out. This was a procedure probably adapted from the Native American use of the chestnuts. Recent medical research suggests that this horse tissue has anti-inflammatory properties.

It was sometimes impossible to wait to take care of the *fang* until a real dentist could be found, so the designated dentist went to work on the patient. Dr. Coosie would have the victim sit down on a stool and instruct him to hold on to the sides and not let go until the tooth was out. "Wait Coosie! what about my allotted bourbon? You gotta let me have it," the patient would plead. The cook obliged, and the cowboy thus acquired a false sense of infallible courage--but it was better than no courage at all.

With his trusty forceps, if he was lucky enough to have such in his possession, or common pliers in hand, coosie would lock onto the cowboy's head with one arm and fasten the pliers onto the bad tooth with his other hand, and p-u-l-l. Sometimes the tooth popped right out, but most of the time it didn't. The patient would be holler'n and trying to get out of the neck hug, but coosie tightened his grip and held on like a bulldog, all the time pulling with all his might.

"Hang on, she's fixing to come loose...hang in there!" Old coosie called on his strength reserves and pulled and twisted those pliers until the poor cowboy felt every bone in his head squeak and grind.

"Damn! What in tarnation do you have in there? A horse's tooth?" By this time, a crowd would have gathered to wince and commiserate with their poor *compadre*.

"Glad it's you, Joe, and not me...."

After what seemed an eternity, the tooth would pull free with roots spread out like giant roots on a tree. "Hardest tooth I ever pulled at," said coosie, wiping the blood off his pliers with an old rag. "I was afraid if I let you up for a spell that you would run away."

The relieved patient would examine the now-extracted source of pain as he happily took his allotted post-operation ration of bourbon to help seal the open wound and prevent infection. Pulling a tooth was definitely classified in the bourbon deserving category.

Cowhands were a tough breed. When they got a deep cut from wire, knives, axes or whatever, they often doctored themselves. They cleaned out the wound with some salt water and wrapped it tight with whatever cloth they could get their hands on. This was a man whose hands were not particularly on the clean side, having been in dust, manure, cow blood from doctoring the cattle, or whatever else.

A couple of days later, he would take off the bandage and let the air and sun get to it, and Mother Nature would dry it up with a hard crust. If the cowboy was lucky, he would not come down with lockjaw or blood poisoning, or even any sort of serious infection. When a cowboy got banged up a bit too much to ride or carry his share of the load, he would stay around the chuck wagon and help out the cook as best he could. After a few days, the poor old soul would be bored stiff with the inactivity, and more than likely feeling better, mounted up and got back into the groove of things. The teasing by the other cowpokes as to his condition and lack of perseverance and mental toughness and such helped get him over whatever ailed him, *muy pronto*. The other cowboys could be pretty hard on a poor old soul.

On the lighter side of things though, one doctor once attributed the often-found bowed legs and lean physique of the cowboy to his calcium-deficient diet. The long hours in the saddle, day in and day out, year after year, likely played a bigger role though.

With the addition of canned tomatoes, came a side medicinal benefit. It seems that the canned tomatoes helped to quench their thirst, and the acidic tomato juice counteracted the ill effects of alkali dust inhaled by the cowboys on the trail, especially those bringing up the rear.

One of the most feared and painful medical situations was attributed to the bite of a rattlesnake. Although the cowboys were careful and knew the way of the snakes, accidents did happen, and once in a while a cowboy would be bitten.

Most boots would protect the cowpoke, but some boot uppers weren't very long, and the striking snake could bite the calf area. Snakes were especially plentiful after a rain had wet down the area. Though a snakebite was not necessarily fatal, it did cause the victim to become deathly ill, and the limb where the bite had taken place would swell up considerably. It wasn't a pretty sight to behold.

While on a cattle drive passing through Foard County up near the Texas panhandle, one of the cowboys was bitten while out gathering firewood. He had reached into a bunch of dried tree limbs and, without warning, the snake, probably startled, struck with its vicious fangs, piercing his forearm.

The cowboy came over to the chuck wagon and told coosie the predicament he was in. He showed the cook where he had been bitten. The two little fang holes on his forearm were evident, and swelling had already begun to set in--it was a frightful sight, already black and blue.

There was no doctor for miles, the nearest community being Crowell some twenty-five miles distant, and there was no assurance even that a doctor would be there. Coosie would have to do the best he could, since there were no known remedies. The cowboy was already deathly sick and was taking the worst of it.

Just about then, a nearby rancher happened to come by and saw the situation and immediately took action. It turned out that one W.W. Melton had a small ranch a short distance down the creek, and he took off a'running as fast as his horse could take him, instructing coosie to keep the victim as comfortable as possible. He would be back with a remedy.

Meanwhile coosie tied a tourniquet just above the young man's elbow, attempting in doing so to delay the poison from spreading up towards the heart. The victim also received a much-needed allotment of bourbon. The cook then proceeded to cut two small cross-cuts at each fang wound, hoping to let some of the poison flow out with the blood.

Young Melton had remembered how as a young boy, his father had been bitten by a copperhead snake. His mother had caught a chicken and split it down the back, and while it was throbbing in its own hot blood, she had wrapped the steaming chicken around the hand where the bite had occurred. The flesh of that chicken had turned an ugly, greenish color where the poison had been literally "sucked" out of his father's hand.

Melton ran and caught the first chicken he could get his hands on and hurried back to the chuck wagon camp. He immediately killed the hen, and with its feathers still on it, split it down the back and wrapped it around the forearm of the cowboy.

Whether it did any good or not, no one could say, but coosie still swears by the remedy...the cowpoke recovered in record time.

From that day on, the remedy was spread out to distant outfits by word-of-mouth and was known as the "Melton snake-bite cure." W.W. Melton also gave coosie a jar of "snake oil" and told him how effective this oil was for the "cure" of rheumatism, which a lot of the older cowboys had due to the rough and tumble life they led. As the cold weather set in, and the old bones began to ache, coosie would take out the "Melton jar" cure--snake oil.

During the spring, when the snakes would come out of hibernation, the cowboys would kill a few of them and bring them over to the cook. Coosie would skin them and cut them up into little chunks and "fry" the pieces in an old frying pan, saving the fat which resulted. Coosie would build up a good supply of the snake fat in a large jar. The "Melton cure" was appreciated very highly by the hands for those painful limbs brought about by the cold winter days.

A rattlesnake could slither into a bedroll to stay warm, and when the cowboy woke up and moved around, the startled snake would bite. Coosie would advise that the cowboys encircle their bedrolls with their lariat, which was supposed to keep the snakes away. Perhaps. Perhaps not. Regardless, many a cowboy swore by this "superstition."

Superstitions held a place in medicine lore of the time. Many trail hands wore vests over their shirts and under their jackets, but never did button up the front of the vest, believing that doing so would keep them too warm and would lead to colds and rheumatism.

One tea-like drink which supposedly helped with upset stomachs was procured from the state of Missouri on one of the early trail drives. This drink also supposedly helped "thin the blood" which was supposed to make for better blood circulation and thus better health. The Sassafras tree produced the dried root which could be carried for long periods of time. This root, boiled in water, produced a sweet-smelling and sweet-tasting drink with medicinal qualities. Most all outfits carried an ample supply of dried sassafras roots in their chuck wagon.

One very simple and readily available cure for a skin burn, and to help the skin heal, was simply to rub the affected area with a slice of raw potato.

Last, but not least, in the medicinal area, was the Mexican influence of the *curanderos*, healers. Many of the cooks had been brought up by their parents believing in and learning the healing properties of plants and herbs for many ailments. A cook fortunate enough to possess some of this *curandero* knowledge was very valuable to the outfit, increasing his stock and power within the camp.

Part 9

WHY TRAIL DRIVES ENDED

The great cowboy experience had begun in 1866 and lasted until shortly after 1885. Its golden age was over--a scant two decades after it had begun. In one generation, the cattle kingdom had spread from Texas to Oklahoma, Kansas, Nebraska, the Dakotas, Wyoming, Nevada, Utah, Montana, Colorado, Arizona, and New Mexico.

The end of the cattle trail drives came with the expansion of the railroads into Texas, barbed wire, overgrazing and overstocking, and the birth of ranches situated closer to the railheads, to provide the needed cattle. In its heyday though, more than eight million longhorns had come up the trails from Texas to the various railheads.

An additional factor of the end of the trail drives was the disastrous winter of 1886-1887. The deadly blizzards with their freezing temperatures killed up to ninety percent of the cattlemen's stock. The ground was so frozen that the cattle could not even paw their way through to any life-sustaining vegetation, and the ranchers could not get feed wagons through the deep snows to feed their stock. There were not enough cattle left alive that spring to drive north to the railheads. Before another year had passed, expanding rail lines and ranches established closer to the old rail destinations eliminated the need for extended cattle drives and hastened the end of that colorful Western period.

Cowboying on big trail drives was now gone forever, but the cowboy stayed on and worked on the large ranches where roundups were still a necessary function. A rancher still needed the cowboy's skills, but now the cowboy found himself a year-'round employee and, much to his dismay, many of his tasks smacked of farming and didn't need a horse to carry them out. The foreman was always on him to do this or do that. The cowboy on the open range and trail, if he knew his work, hardly ever got any orders from anyone...he had been pretty much his own boss.

Gone, like a tumbleweed in the wind, was the cowboy's sense of freedom and individuality that defined his way of life. He had been accustomed to an unrestricted, carefree life on the plains with lots of challenges and adventure. The new ways were quite predictable, repetitious, and unappealing. They contrasted sharply with the life on the trail he had become accustomed to.

As history has captured them, the color, the adventure, the drama, the camaraderie, the humor...all of these overshadow the tedium, the discomforts, the monotonous and dangerous work that accompanied the trail drives. And at the center of it all was the chuck wagon with its picaresque empresario, the cocinero.

Of course, none of this tremendous migration could have happened without the cowboy, the way he lived--or the way people thought he lived. He rode down the trail, following coosie in his wagon, to forever become a part of our American heritage.

GLOSSARY

Airtights: Colloquial term for canned goods; at the time usually limited to corn, peaches, tomatoes, and milk.

Arbuckle's Brand: famous coffee brand of the period preferred by cowboys.

Asado: Beef meat roasted over an open camp fire.

Bait: Another word for food, as used by the cowboys.

Bandanna: Handkerchief cloth used by cowboys as a general purpose wash cloth, filter, dust mask, etc.

Baquero: Mexican word for cowboy. Variant of *vaquero* or buckaroo.

Bean Master: Colloquial term for cook.

Belly-wash: Weak coffee.

Biscuit Roller: Colloquial term for cook.

Blackstrap: The thick, black kind of molasses.

Buckaroo: Anglicized word for *vaquero* or cowboy. Used more in the northern states. Southern states use *vaquero* or cowboy.

Cana: Sugar cane. Also sugarcane liquor.

Canned Cow: Colloquial term for canned milk.

Caporal: Mexican word for ranch foreman or roundup boss.

Carne Seca: Mexican term for dried beef or beef jerky.

Chaps: Leather leggings worn to protect the cowboy's legs. *Chaparreras* or *chapas* for short.

Chuck: Colloquial term for food, grub, chow.

Chuck Wagon Chicken: Humorous word for fried bacon.

Chuck-Line Rider: Unemployed cowboy who rode from one ranch to another, exchanging news and gossip for a free meal.

Cinch: A strap used to hold the saddle on a horse. Mexican word is *cincha*.

Cocinero: Camp cook, anglicized to coosie.

Coffee: *Cafe* as it is known to Mexicans. Cowboys wanted a strong cup with lots of caffeine, strong and thick, and very hot--the hotter the better.

Compadre: Mexican word meaning friend, companion, pardner. Also one who baptized another's baby infant. *Comadre* was the female version.

Coosie: Colloquial anglicized term for *cocinero*.

Cow grease: Butter.

Cow juice: Milk. Mexican word is *leche*.

Cut straw and molasses: Real poor food; better than nothing.

Dally: Term for a rope technique which was derived from the Mexican word *dar la vuelta,* to give it a turn.

Dry camp: A camp without any water, which was tough on the cook.

Dulce: The Mexican word for candy or sweet.

Dutch Oven: Cast-iron pot with lid used to cook food over coals and open fires. The most popular pot used by the cook. Has three short "legs" to hold it off the ground to allow the hot coals to be placed in-between.

Eating Irons: Colloquial word for silverware.

Espuelas: Mexican word for spurs.

Estribo: Mexican term for stirrup. Also *estrigo*.

Fixins: The term for tobacco and the thin-soft paper used to roll cigarettes. Also could mean having the items to cook a particular dish.

Frijoles: Mexican dried pinto beans, sometimes called Mexican strawberries by the cowboys.

Grub: Colloquial word meaning food.

Grub Pile!: Call to eat.

Grub Slinger: Colloquial for cook. Also grubworm, grub spoiler.

Hacienda: Mexican word for a large ranch, estate.

Hen Fruit: Eggs.

Hombre: Mexican word for man.

Jaquima: Mexican term anglicized to hackamore, headstall, halter.

Java: Colloquial for coffee.

Jerky: Dried meat. Derived from the Mexican word *charqui*.

Jinete: Mexican word for cowboy who breaks horses.

Lariat: Rope. Anglicized from the word *la reata*.

Latigo: Anglicized to latigo. A leather strap which holds saddle on horse.

Lick: Colloquial term for molasses or syrup.

Love Apples: Colloquial term for canned tomatoes.

Makings: Same as "fixings." Tobacco and paper used to roll cigarettes.

"Man-at-the-pot!" Yelled at any cowboy who is refilling his cup and now is obliged to go around and fill all the cups held out to him

Montura : Mexican word for saddle.

Night Hawk: A cowboy who watches the horses (*remuda*) at night. Also know as the night wrangler.

Night Guard: A cowboy who watches the trail herd at night.

Padding out his belly: cowboy who eats anything, anytime.

Patron: Mexican word used to refer to the owner of the ranch or *hacienda*.

Pooch: A sweet dish made out of canned tomatoes, bread, and sugar. Was said to have been good for sick cowboys.

Pot Luck: A meal made up of whatever coosie could rustle up.

Pot Rustler: One of many words used to describe the cook.

Prairie oysters: Calf's testicles. Also called mountain oysters.

Quarta: Mexican word for quirt, whip.

Ranchero: Mexican word which was anglicized to rancher.

Rancho: Mexican word which was anglicized to ranch.

Reata: Rope. Anglicized the Mexican word *la reata* to lariat.

Remuda: Horses used by the cowboys. Tended by the horse wrangler.

Rodeo: Anglicized to rodeo. A Mexican term for a roundup.

Segundo: Second in command, the straw boss on a trail drive.

Skunk Eggs: Colloquial word for onions.

Soogan: Also sougan which is a heavy woven blanket used in bed rolls.

Son-of-a-bitch Stew: Also known in mixed company as son-of-a-gun stew. A concoction of the beef's innards such as the liver, heart, tripe, tongue, sweetbreads, etc. used in cooking a stew favored by cowboys.

Sop: Greasy gravy.

Sourdough: Fermented flour mixture used as a starter for camp bread and biscuits. Also a colloquial word for the cook.

Spotted pup: Rice, sugar, cinnamon, and raisins boiled together.

Stretching' the blanket: Colloquial term for telling a tall tale around the campfire.

Sudadero: Mexican word for a horse blanket used under the saddle. Meaning to catch the sweat.

Supper: The main heavy evening meal of the cowboy. Called dinner by non-cowboys.

Tapaderas: Leather coverings that protected the feet by hanging over and below the stirrups.

Trail Boss: The cowboy in charge of the trail drive.

Vaca: Mexican word for cow.

Vamoose: To leave quickly. From the Mexican word *Vamos*.

Vaquero: Mexican working cowboy. The origin of the anglicized word buckaroo.

Wagon Boss: Cowboy in charge of the roundup.

Wipe: Colloquial term for handkerchief or bandanna.

Wrangle: To care for and to drive the horses.

Wrangler: The cowboy who tended the outfit's horses. From the Mexican word *caballerango*.

WORKS CITED

Arnold, Sam'l P. *Eating Up the Santa Fe Trail.*
　　　Colorado University Press of Colorado, 1990.
Beckstead, James H. Cowboying: *A Tough Job in a*
　　　Hard Land. Salt Lake City: University of Utah
　　　Press, 1991.
Brown, Dale. *American Cooking.* New York,
　　　Time-Life Books, 1970.
Brown, Dee. *The American West.* New York:　Charles
　　　Scribner's & Sons, 1994.
Brown,　Mark H. and W.R. Felton. *Before Barbed*
　　　Wire.　New York: Bramhall House, 1956.
Cano, Tony and Ann Sochat. *Echoes in the Wind.* El
　　　Paso, Texas: Reata Publishing, 1994.
Cano, Tony and Ann Sochat. *Dutch Oven Cooking*
　　　with Tony Cano. El Paso, Texas: Reata
　　　Publishing, 1993.
Cartledge, Wayne. Various conversations with author,
　　　Marfa, Texas,　1969-70.
Chilton, Charles. *The Book of the West.* Indianapolis,
　　　New York: Bobbs-Merrill, 1962.
Connor, Seymour V. *A Beggers Chronicle.* Lubbock:
　　　Texas　Technological College, 1961.
Davis, William C. *The American Frontier.* New
　　　York:　Smithmark, 1992.

Ellison, Glenn "Slim" R. *Cowboys Under the Mogollon Rim*. Tucson: University of Arizona Press, 1968.

Forbis, William H. *The Cowboys*. New York: Time Life Books, 1973.

Gard, Wayne. *The Chisholm Trail.* Norman: University of Oklahoma Press, 1954.

Haley, Evetts, J. *Charles Goodnight Cowman & Plainsman.*Norman : University of Oklahoma Press.

Holden, William Curry. *The Espuela Land and Cattle Company*. Austin: Texas State Historical Association.

Kemp, Ben W. with J. C. Dykes. *Cow Dust and Saddle Leather*. Norman: University of Oklahoma Press, 1968.

Kusinitz, Marc. *Folk Medicine.* New York: Chelsea House, 1992.

Marrin, Albert. *Cowboys, Indians, and Gunfighters.* New York: Maxwell Macmillan International, 1993.

Melton, W.W. *Stories from Life*. Dallas: Helms, 1949.

Morgan, Sarah. *The Saga of Texas Cookery*. Austin: The Encino Press, 1973.

Potter, Edgar "Frosty" R. *Cowboy Slang.* Golden West, 1986.

Reedstrom, Ernest Lisle. *Historic Dress of The Old West*. Poole, New York, Sydney: Blandford Press, 1986.

Seidman, Laurence I. *Once in the Saddle*. New York: Facts on file, 1973, 1991.

Sewell, Linck and Joyce Gibson Roach. *A Folk History of Texas Foods*. Fort Worth: Texas Christian University Press, 1989.

Shawver, Lona. *Chuck Wagon Windies*. San Antonio: The Naylor Company, 1950.

Sims, Judge Orland L. *Cowpokes, Nesters, & So Forth*. Austin: The Encino Press, 1970.

Slatta, Richard W. *Cowboys of the Americas*. New Haven: Yale University Press, 1990.

Slatta, Richard W. *The Cowboy Encyclopedia*. Santa Barbara: ABC-CLIO, 1994.

Sullivan, Dulcie. *The LS Brand*. Austin & London: University of Texas Press, 1968.

Ward, Fay E. *The Cowboy at Work*. Norman and London: University of Oklahoma Press.

Ward, Don. *Cowboys and Cattle Country*. New York: American Heritage, 1961.

West, John O. *Cowboy Folk Humor*. Little Rock: August House, 1990.

Worthington, Patricia H. *"...but it tasted good to us."* Diss. The University of Texas at El Paso,1974.